The Stuff
That Dreams
Are Made On

Also by Clifton Snider

Jesse Comes Back (1976)
Bad Smoke   Good Body (1980)
Jesse and His Son (1982)
Edwin: A Character in Poems (1984)
Blood & Bones (1988)
Impervious to Piranhas (1989)

The Stuff
That Dreams
Are Made On

A Jungian
Interpretation
of Literature

Clifton Snider

Chiron Publications
Wilmette, Illinois

The Chiron Monograph Series, Volume V
General Editors: Nathan Schwartz-Salant and Murray Stein
Managing Editor: Siobhan Drummond

Grateful acknowledgment is made to the following:
Lady Lever Art Gallery, Port Sunlight, England, for permission to reproduce *The Beguiling of Merlin* by Edward Burne-Jones.

Western Kentucky University, Bowling Green, Kentucky, for permission to reprint, in revised form, "Merlin in Victorian Poetry: A Jungian Analysis" which first appeared in *The Victorian Newsletter* (Fall 1987).

Tate Gallery, London/Art Resource, New York, for permission to reproduce *Queen Guenevere* or *La Belle Iseult* by William Morris.

The Trustees, the Cecil Higgins Art Gallery, Bedford, England, for permission to reproduce *Paolo and Francesca* by D. G. Rossetti.

Permissions continued on page 160

Library of Congress Catalog Card Number: 90-40181

Printed in the United States of America.
Editing and book design by Siobhan Drummond

Library of Congress Cataloging-in-Publication Data:

Snider, Clifton.
   The stuff that dreams are made on : a Jungian interpretation of literature / Clifton Snider.
      p.   cm. — (Chiron mongraph series ; v. 5)
   Includes bibliographical references and index.
   ISBN 0-933029-37-3
      1. English literature — 19th century — History and criticism — Theory, etc. 2. English literature — 20th century — History and criticism — Theory, etc. 3. Jung, C.G. (Carl Gustav), 1875-1961 — Influence. 4. American literature — History and criticism — Theory, etc. 5. Archetype (Psychology) in literature. I. Title.
   II. Series.
   PR468.A72S65 1991
   809'.93353 — dc20
                                                                      90-40181
                                                                      CIP

ISBN 0-933029-37-3

To my mother and
to the memory
of my father

Bare-footed, she slithers above him,
his book of magic held like a platter,
a phallic body, feline fingers,
phallic nose, feminine lips,

her neck an enormous temptation,
snakes on her head, her dress a swirl —
blue-green skin, sadistic red hair:
she's the one for him.

Gray-haired Merlin has lost his beard,
sick with disappointment: gaunt, weak
tomcat eyes, a young man's fingers,
he wants her to want him again.

She took his wisdom & will —
excitement in the forest,
the overwhelming white flowers.
The hawthorn tree envelops him.

Clifton Snider,
"The Beguiling of Merlin"

Contents

Preface

When I first became interested in applying Jungian theory to literature in the early seventies, very few book-length studies existed. There were Morris Philipson's *Outline of a Jungian Aesthetics* (Northwestern University Press, 1963) and Alex Aronson's *Psyche and Symbol in Shakespeare* (Indiana University Press, 1972). Today, book-length studies by Bettina L. Knapp, Martin Bickman, and many others are available.* New books about Jung's analytical psychology, new clinical applications of his work, and new selections of Jung's writings appear frequently.

My goal in this study has been to present Carl Jung's theories in a manner accessible to students of literature, although I hope Jungian specialists will find my comments valuable, too. I present not only Jung's theories about the conscious and unconscious mind, but also his neo-Platonic theories about creativity. These I try to apply, again accessibly, to important literature of the nineteenth and twentieth centuries in Britain and America.

This present volume represents years of thought and research. Much is new and much has appeared in earlier published versions. The *Psychocultural Review* (and later, Joseph Natoli's *Psychological Perspectives on Literature*) published earlier versions of Chapter One, in which I introduce Jungian concepts. The *Psychocultural Review* also published a version of my chapter on Swinburne's *Tristram of Lyonesse*. I have to thank Joseph Natoli for asking me to write a new application of Jungian theory to literature. This resulted in my interpretation of *The Member of the Wedding*, especially challenging from a Jungian viewpoint because Jungian psychology tends to focus on the second half of life. Discovering psychological insights in a novel about an adolescent girl written during World War II was particularly rewarding.

Chapter Two focuses on an archetypal figure, Merlin, in nineteenth-century British literature. Jung believed that archetypal images appear when the individual or the collective psyche most needs them to correct

---

*Knapp's books are called *A Jungian Approach to Literature* (Southern Illinois University Press, 1984) and *Women in Twentieth-Century Literature: A Jungian View* (Pennsylvania State University Press, 1987). Bickman's is *American Romantic Psychology: Emerson, Poe, Whitman, Dickinson, Melville* (Spring Publications, 1988). H. R. Coursen has written a new Jungian interpretation of Shakespeare: *The Compensatory Psyche: A Jungian Approach to Shakespeare* (University Press of America, 1986); and June Singer has written *The Unholy Bible: Blake, Jung and the Collective Unconscious* (Sigo, 1986). For the student, scholar, or critic who wishes to pursue Jungian studies of literature, I recommend the newly published *Jungian Literary Criticism, 1920–1980* (Scarecrow, 1988), a highly opinionated but nevertheless useful annotated bibliography of Jungian criticism for the years indicated in the title.

psychic imbalance. Victorian society, like our own, was spiritually, morally, and psychically split. A symbol of wholeness—of what Jung calls the Self—such as Merlin helps to right the imbalance in a positive way. Sometimes the archetypal images mirror contemporary imbalance. This is what happened when Oscar Wilde wrote *The Picture of Dorian Gray*, which reflects the moral and spiritual schizophrenia of the late Victorian era as it does our own era, and that is why I chose to analyze it here.

More positive examples of what Jung calls "visionary" literature (literature that stems from the collective unconscious and intends thus to right contemporary psychic imbalance) are *Tristram of Lyonesse*, Virginia Woolf's *Orlando* and *The Waves*, and Carson McCullers's *Clock Without Hands*, a novel which deserves more attention than it has received. All of these pieces are examples of the individuation process that leads to wholeness or the archetypal Self. W. H. Auden, perhaps the greatest poet in English from the generation following Yeats, Eliot, and Frost, made the healing archetype of love the central theme of his life's work, and I include a rather brief analysis of Auden's work as my final chapter.

Obviously I could have chosen other nineteenth- and twentieth-century authors whose work compensates for collective imbalance in a Jungian way. My choices do reflect my own taste, but they are, I feel, particularly representative of their periods. Tennyson and Swinburne offer contrasting responses to similar legendary material, both working out their own archetypal solutions to the Victorian crisis of faith, the secular versus the spiritual. Wilde, England's only major playwright of the 1890s and a writer whose work epitomizes that decade, created in Dorian Gray a character whose schizophrenia reflects the moral hypocrisy of the day.

Virginia Woolf was a child of the Victorian era with all its sexism, prudery, and loss of faith. Her treatment of androgyny in *Orlando* and *The Waves* offers psychic solutions to sexism and prudery. And through her unconscious depiction of Jung's individuation process, Woolf also offers a psychic solution to the loss of faith in traditional religion. The same is true for Carson McCullers, writing in the generation after Woolf, one torn, nevertheless, by international crises and war. W. H. Auden, the only one of these authors actually to have read Jung, as far as we know, addresses contemporary psychic imbalance (reflected, for example, in war, prejudice, the need for individual growth, and the threat of nuclear holocaust) and offers love as an archetype of wholeness. Taken together, the work of these authors is a kind of psychic history of the past 150 years.

Jung writes that the artist is a person "upon whom a heavier burden is laid than upon ordinary mortals" ("Psychology and Literature," *CW* 15, pp. 102–103). However romantic this may sound, and however true it may be, Jung emphasized that a biographical approach to literature misses its collective appeal — its archetypal appeal, the "re-immersion in the state of *participation mystique* [which] is the secret of artistic creation" (p. 105). This is why I do not attempt to analyze the lives of these authors. Rather, I analyze their work in their contemporary contexts to show how that work compensates for collective psychic imbalance.

Acknowledgments

I wish to thank the editors of the journals where portions of my analyses were first published in earlier versions. In addition to the *Psychocultural Review* and Joseph Natoli's book, these journals include *Modern Fiction Studies*, which published a version of my interpretation of *Orlando* (1979), and *The Markham Review*, which published a version of my interpretation of *Clock Without Hands* (1982). *American Imago* published my short article on Auden's "Lady Weeping at the Crossroads" and "Atlantis" (1982), and *The Victorian Newsletter* published my article on "Merlin in Victorian Poetry" (1987).

I would especially like to thank Edward Mendelson, Auden's literary executor, who has allowed me to publish a letter I received from Auden in April of 1972. I would like also to thank the Huntington Library, San Marino, California, for their help in researching Merlin. Nigel Nicolson and Joanne Trautmann allowed me, on July 9, 1977, at Sissinghurst Castle, Kent, to read the proofs for the then-unpublished third volume of *The Letters of Virginia Woolf*. Over the years, many others have encouraged and inspired me in my studies of the authors included in this book and of Jung. These include the following, whom I wish to thank here, hoping I have not forgot any others I ought to thank: Kenneth Ames, Harold Aspiz, Gary Barricklow, A. Robert Bell, Martin Bickman, Mary Brennan, Edith Buchanan, Paul Davis, Morris Eaves, Norma L. Goodrich, Robert Fleming, William H. Jackson, David Johnson, Lee M. Johnson, Robert A. Johnson, Eileen Lothamer, Ivan Melada, Robert Peters, Audrey Peterson, Merlin Snider, Mark Thompson, Paul Trachtenberg, John Williams, Hugh Witemeyer, and Joseph Zavadil. I am indebted also to the late Christopher Isherwood. My deep appreciation goes to Murray Stein for his faith in this project and to Siobhan Drummond Granner, who helped midwife it to publication. I would particularly like to thank Dr. Andrew Berner, who first pointed out the puer archetype to me, and Dr. John Talley, a Jungian analyst, with whom I studied as a graduate student in the early seventies. I also would like to thank Dr. Karl W. E. Anatol, Dean of the School of Humanities, California State University, Long Beach, and Dr. Arthur Axelrad, Chair of the Department of English, for their encouragement. Last, I am indebted to my students, especially to those in two courses I taught on archetypes for the Honors Program at California State University, Long Beach, and to those in a Virginia Woolf seminar, which I taught in the spring of 1987.

Chapter One

Jungian Theory and
Its Literary Application

We are such stuff
As dreams are made on, and our little life
Is rounded with a sleep.
Shakespeare, *The Tempest*

Although Freud's psychoanalysis remains the most influential psychology in literary criticism, Jung's analytical psychology has exerted, within the past decade or two, a growing force among literary critics. Part of this renaissance of interest in Jung has been due to negative responses to the Freudian view of literature as the expression of the artist's neurosis; but the rise of Jungian criticism also parallels the rise of "archetypal criticism," which is, itself, influenced heavily by Jungian thought. Indeed, Jungian literary criticism is sometimes placed as a subcategory of archetypal or "myth" criticism. René Wellek lists six major kinds of criticism "new in this last half-century"; one of these is "psychoanalytic criticism," while another is "myth criticism appealing to the results of cultural anthropology and the speculation of Carl Jung" (1961, p. 103). Jung's influence on archetypal or myth criticism may be seen in the wealth of recent anthologies of literature that are concerned wholly or in part with works of an archetypal nature. In addition, an increasing number of dissertations, articles, and books are using Jungian psychology to illuminate literature.

The most thorough treatment of Jungian ideas about art is Morris Philipson's *Outline of a Jungian Aesthetic*. Philipson maintains that it would appear that of Jung's literary modes only the visionary is worth considering from a psychological point of view because the psychological mode is already clearly intelligible. Yet "Jung has oversimplified his scheme for the modes of art and their interpretation" (Philipson 1963, p. 160), for there is an unconscious element in the seemingly conscious psychological mode and a conscious shaping in the apparently unconscious visionary mode. If Jung is a bit inconsistent in his classification of literary types, Philipson's justification for studying art ("visionary" art in particular) is clear: "Jung believes symbolical [i.e., visionary] artwork serves the same purpose for a society that an individual symbolic experience [as in a dream, for example] serves for a patient in therapy" (ibid., pp. 127–128). Thus, the questions Jungian literary criticism attempts to answer are: "What *purpose* does the symbolic work of art fulfill in the psychic life of a society? What is its psychic significance?" (ibid., p. 127). We may also say that once we have answered these questions we shall have a greater appreciation for how a particular piece of literature *works*. Further, as Philipson writes,

> Jung offers a basis for a historical analysis of psychically significant works of art. "The nature of the work of art (Jung says) permits conclusions to be drawn concerning the character of the period from which it sprang." Consequently, a psychological interpretation can be offered in answer to such questions as: "What was the significance of realism and naturalism to their age? What was the meaning of romanticism, or Hellenism? They were tendencies of art which brought to the surface that unconscious element of which the contemporary mental atmosphere had most need. The artist as educator of his time — much could be said about that today." (Ibid., p. 130)

Strictly speaking, the psychology of Carl Gustav Jung should be called "analytical psychology" in order to distinguish it from Sigmund Freud's "psychoanalysis" and Alfred Adler's "individual psychology." Jung, who was associated as a young man with Freud, feels that the theories of both Freud and Adler are reductive. Freud reduces neurosis to sexual repression (the "pleasure principle"); Adler reduces mental illness to the drive for power stemming from the inferiority complex (Jung 1934a, p. 39). Jung posits a theory of human psychology that essentially traces mental problems to an imbalance of psychic forces within the individual. His theory is as applicable to "normal" human development as to the "abnormal"; it rests on a concept of development that progresses by stages, each of which is determined by a particular instinctual "archetypal" constellation.

Like Freud, Jung believes in a personal unconscious that contains all the repressed and forgotten or even subliminal perceptions of the individual. But Jung goes a step beyond Freud to postulate the collective unconscious. The collective unconscious contains the archetypes that are, like physical instincts, the innate ability and tendency to create forms and images. These images are symbols of the archetype. Archetypes are, by definition, common to all human beings, and their number is immeasurable. In the same way, archetypal images are infinitely varied. In this sense Jung's theory is not reductive.

The archetype is only an hypothesis. It cannot be proved; nor can we ever fully know the meaning of an archetype. We do know, however, that the central characteristic of the archetype is its duality: it always contains the potential to have both positive and negative effects. Within the individual, the archetype is stirred to produce images or symbols whenever an imbalance in the psyche is struck. Thus, the archetype exhibits a peculiar autonomy. The individual may then have archetypal (as opposed to merely personal) dreams and fantasies that are trying to compensate for the imbalance. The same applies to communities (which always have a collective consciousness). If a large group of people have an imbalance in their collective consciousness or their collective unconscious, then archetypal images will appear in myths, in folk tales, and in more formal literature.

Literary criticism based on Jungian analytical psychology can add a new dimension to literary art. It can show, as I have indicated, how literature contributes to the psychic balance of a community. Examining a literary work in Jungian terms can show why the piece is structured as it is. For example (as I will demonstrate in a later chapter), the passage in Algernon Charles Swinburne's longest and most ambitious poem, *Tristram of Lyonesse*, where Tristram jumps naked into the sea, has been criticized for being "an especially long digression" (Maynadier 1907, p. 374). From a Jungian point of view, however, this passage is crucial to the poem, for it represents Tristram's last realization of the Self (psychic wholeness) before he dies. In the sea, Tristram is at one with nature and himself. The naked dip in the sea is the third time that Tristram is able to unite the opposing parts of his psyche.[1] The fourth, and most complete, realization of wholeness for Tristram is his death; and, since in Jung's theory four is the number of wholeness, the sea-dip episode is absolutely essential and necessary from a Jungian point of view. The structure of the poem would not be complete without it.

It may be objected that some inferior works are archetypal and, like great art, also compensate for imbalance. This is quite true, but a Jungian literary critic will not give such works much attention.[2] The critic who employs Jungian psychology cannot operate in isolation. He needs the tools of other schools of criticism to determine the value of a piece of art. What Ronald Crane has to say about his neo-Aristotelean school of criticism expresses exactly my sentiments about Jungian criticism: "I should not want to leave the impression . . . that I think it the only mode of criticism seriously worth cultivation at the present time by either teachers of literature or critics, but simply that its development, along with the others, might have many fruitful consequences for our teaching and criticism generally" (1953, p. 191). The value of Jungian criticism is that it sets literature in its proper place in a human context as a representative of the psyche without, at the same time, getting away from literature's intrinsic worth as an art form.

Since I am dealing with Jungian theory as a tool of literary criticism, perhaps it is advisable to distinguish first Jung's concept of the archetype from that of the major "archetypal" literary theorist, Northrop Frye. Frye defines archetype as "a symbol which connects one poem with another and thereby helps to unify and integrate our literary experience" (1957, p. 99). By limiting archetypes to literature, Frye reduces their universality. A Jungian critic, on the other hand, recognizes that the archetypal image found in literature also forms part of a huge complex of images and symbols that have psychic meaning for all people. He does not, however, have to go outside the literature itself, except for his terms and his theory — and this is what any critic does anyway, including Frye. Frye's theory of literary modes is as much "outside" of literature, to the extent that it is Frye's own creation, as is Jung's theory of literary modes. This fact does not in the least diminish the validity or the utility of either theory. The Jungian critic looks at an archetype in a particular piece of literature *in the context of the work in front of him*, just as a Jungian psychiatrist interprets his patient's dream in the context of the patient's individual experience, situation, and psychological condition.

Jung used the terms "motifs" and "primordial images" to stand for "archetypes." For Jung, "primordial" means "archaic," or "in striking accord with familiar mythological motifs" (1921, p. 443). He says that the archetype is always collective; that is, "it is at least common to entire peoples or epochs. In all probability the most important mythological motifs are common to all times and races" (ibid., p. 443). Elsewhere, Jung has said that "archetypes appear in myths and fairy tales just as they do in dreams and in the products of psychotic fantasy" (Jung and Kerényi 1963, p. 72). And they also appear in formal literature. Furthermore, Jung writes, "contents of an archetypal character are manifestations of processes in the collective unconscious. Hence they do not refer to anything that is or has been conscious, but to something essentially unconscious. In the last analysis, therefore, it is impossible to say what they refer to. . . . The ultimate core of meaning may be circumscribed, but not described" (ibid., p. 75). If the archetype itself is not conscious, its symbols (which may be called archetypal images) are brought to consciousness in myths, dreams, and so forth.

Jung continually revised his idea of the archetype as new evidence presented itself. For a good review of this development, I suggest Jolande Jacobi's *Complex/Archetype/Symbol* (1959). Jung's essay in *Man and His Symbols* represents his final statement on the archetype:

> The term "archetype" is often misunderstood as meaning certain definite mythological images or motifs. But these are nothing more than conscious representations; it would be absurd to assume that such variable representations could be inherited.
>
> *The archetype is a tendency to form such representations of a motif* — representations that can vary a great deal in detail without losing their basic pattern. There are, for instance, many representations of the motif of the hostile brethren, but the motif remains the same. (Jung et al. 1964, p. 67, italics mine)

Jung goes on to defend himself against critics who "assumed I am dealing with 'inherited representations.' " Archetypes are, indeed, "an instinctive *trend*, as marked as the impulse of birds to build nests, or ants to form organized colonies" (ibid., pp. 67–69). One contemporary Jungian, Edward F. Edinger, has said: "An archetype is to the psyche what an instinct is to the body" (1968, p. 6). Although archetypal criticism has been called reductive by some critics who are largely unfamiliar with it, in fact it recognizes the infinite possibilities for the expression of archetypes (which are themselves unlimited). If the shadow is an archetype of the unconscious, there are at least as many varieties of its archetypal image as there are human individuals; and the likelihood of a similar diversity of "motifs" is just as great.

Even though the number of archetypes is limitless, they can be classified to some extent. Jung says that the shadow, the anima, and the animus are "the archetypes most clearly characterized from the empirical point of view," and that they "have the most frequent and the most disturbing influence on the ego" (1951, p. 8). Elsewhere, he has listed as major archetypes: the wise old man, the child, the mother, the maiden, as well as the three just mentioned (Jung and Kerényi 1963, p. 157). As we shall see, there are also archetypal themes or patterns.

At this point, however, I would like to discuss Jung's theory of creativity and the artist and how it relates to his theory of the archetype and to literary criticism. For Jung, the artist, or at least the superior artist, does not, as Freud believes, create from the repressed contents of his own personal unconscious; rather, he gives form (or image) to the archetypes of the collective unconscious. The poet "lifts the idea he is seeking to express out of the occasional and the transitory into the realm of the ever-enduring. He transmutes our personal destiny into the destiny of mankind, and evokes in us all those beneficent forces that ever and anon have enabled humanity to find refuge from every peril and to outlive the longest night" (Jung 1931a, p. 82). Just as the archetypal, as opposed to the merely personal, dreams of an individual are compensatory, so great art "is constantly at work educating the spirit of the age, conjuring up the forms which the age is most lacking" (ibid.). Great literature, then, speaks to its era to correct the latter's psychic imbalance.

When he talks about the artist and literature, Jung makes it clear he speaks from a psychologist's point of view, not from a literary critic's standpoint. He is most interested in the creative process, and his views on this are not wholly unique, having been suggested as far back as Plato (in his theory of inspiration in *Ion*). The creative act is, essentially, an "autonomous complex," and it springs from the unconscious: "The unborn work in the psyche of the artist is a force of nature that achieves its end either with tyrannical might or with the subtle cunning of nature herself, quite regardless of the personal fate of the man who is its vehicle" (Jung 1931a, p. 75). Therefore, it is a mistake to analyze a work of art strictly on the basis of the artist's biography or personal psychology, for if these ever fully explain the work of art, then it is reduced merely to a symptom and is not worth further study (ibid., p. 86). This, of course, is contrary to the view of Freud's school of psychoanalysis.

In "Psychology and Literature" (1950), Jung classifies literature into two modes: the "psychological," which springs from the conscious mind, and the "visionary," which springs from the collective unconscious. The first mode requires little psychological interpretation, for it is readily explainable in itself, its "raw material" having been "derived from the contents of man's consciousness, from his eternally repeated joys and sorrows, but clarified and transfigured by the poet." In this group belong "all the novels dealing with love, the family milieu, crime and society, together with didactic poetry, the greater number of lyrics, and drama both tragic and comic" (Jung 1950, p. 89). Jung is, of course, speaking as a psychologist, and has earlier stated that sometimes psychologists are most interested in works "of highly dubious merit" (ibid., p. 88). His classification is, then, a little naive from the literary critic's point of view.

This is Jung's definition of the visionary mode: "It is something strange that derives its existence from the hinterland of man's mind, as if it had emerged from the abyss of prehuman ages, or from a superhuman world of contrasting light and darkness. It is a primordial experience which surpasses man's understanding and to which in his weakness he may easily succumb" (Jung 1950, p. 90). Jung uses Goethe's *Faust* to illustrate the difference between his modes. The first part of *Faust* is psychological, the second visionary. Other examples of works in the second category are: *Shepherd of Hermas*, Dante; Wagner's *Ring*, *Tristan*, and *Parsifal*; William Blake's paintings and poetry; E. T. A. Hoffman's *The Gold Bowl*; and James Joyce's *Ulysses*, although in his essay on *Ulysses*, Jung expresses some reservations (1950, p. 91, 1934b, pp. 109–134).

In "Psychology and Literature," Jung refutes the Freudian method of analyzing literature as the expression of neurosis, or at least of the artist's own repressions, by saying something that most critics would agree with (except for, perhaps, the romantic critic who emphasizes the role of the artist's personality): "The essence of a work of art is not to be found in the personal idiosyncrasies that creep into it—indeed, the more there are of them, the less it is a work of art—but in its rising above the personal and speaking from the mind and heart of the artist to the mind and heart of mankind" (1950, p. 101). Jung goes on to echo the Platonic view: "Art is a kind of innate drive that seizes a human being and makes him its instrument" (ibid.). The artist is really two people: the person himself or herself and the artist. Sometimes the creative energy of the artist alters the personal ego of the person so that such things as "ruthlessness, selfishness ('autoeroticism'), vanity, and other infantile traits" may result. The artist "must pay dearly for the divine gift of creative fire"; he is "a man upon whom a heavier burden is laid than upon ordinary mortals" (ibid., pp. 102–103).

The creative process itself has something of the "feminine" in it, arising as it does from the unconscious, "from the realm of the Mothers." The artistic work is organic; "it grows out of . . . [the artist] as a child its mother" (ibid., p. 103). Thus it is that the literary artist creates symbols and archetypal images from the collective unconscious.

Mario Jacoby, in "The Analytical Psychology of C. G. Jung and the Problem of Literary Evaluation," implies that it is "the archetype of the highest good with its unconscious call to action" that motivates the literary critic (1969, p. 124), who is himself a kind of artist—or at least, as Matthew Arnold suggests, a kind of creator. Even if literary critics are not aware of it, they are moved by archetypes.

For Jung the ego is directly attached to consciousness. In *Psychological Types*, he defines the term "consciousness" as the

> function or activity which maintains the relation of psychic contents to the ego. Consciousness is not identical with the psyche . . . because the psyche represents the totality of all psychic contents, and these are not necessarily all directly connected with the ego, i.e., related to it in such a way that they take on the quality of consciousness. (1921, pp. 421–422)

Just as there is a collective unconscious, so there is a collective consciousness common to large groups of people.

Jung defines ego "as the complex factor to which all conscious contents are related. It forms, as it were, the centre of the field of consciousness; and, in so far as this comprises the empirical personality, the ego is the subject of all personal acts of consciousness" (1951, p. 3). He is careful to point out that the ego is not the same as the Self,[3] "since the ego is only the subject of my consciousness, while the self is the subject of my total psyche, which also includes the unconscious" (Jung 1921, p. 425). Furthermore, "The ego is a complex datum which is constituted first of all by a general awareness of your body, of your existence, and secondly by your memory data; you have a certain idea of having been, a long series of memories" (Jung 1968, p. 10). The ego acts as a sort of filter between the unconscious and the conscious, for, as Jacobi says: "All the experience of the outer and inner world must pass through our ego in order to be perceived" (1968, p. 8). Thus, Jung declares that "the ego rests on the *total field of consciousness* and . . . on the *sum total of unconscious contents*," and that "although its bases are in themselves relatively unknown and unconscious, the ego is a conscious factor par excellence" (1951, pp. 4–5). Jung also notes that the ego is not the same as the fields of consciousness and unconsciousness, but that it is the former's "point of reference."

In modern literature, the technique of "stream of consciousness" attempts, as M. H. Abrams says, to "reproduce the raw flow of consciousness, with its perceptions, thought, judgments, feelings, associations, and memories" (1957, p. 60). It should be noted, however, that much of what (in the work of James Joyce and Virginia Woolf, for example) is called "stream of consciousness" is really concerned with the threshold of consciousness, and the contents presented are often below that threshold. That is, the ego often has nothing to do with the "stream" of impressions. The "interior monologue," such as Joyce uses at the end of *Ulysses*, is closer to consciousness in the sense Jung defines the term because the ego is directly involved; it is "conscious" of what is going on.

Jung's definition of ego raises the question of motivation. How well can one's ego perceive why it does something? It may be aware of conscious reasons, but the unconscious ones remain hidden until they pass, as it were, through the ego into consciousness. When, in *The Canterbury Tales*, Chaucer's Pardoner arrogantly proclaims, "I preche nothying but for coveitise," he is only partly right; he is speaking merely from conscious data. There are unconscious reasons that have caused him, via his ego, to cheat the poor, ignorant people. Perhaps subliminally he has felt rejected by these very people and others (he certainly is no favorite among the Canterbury pilgrims) on account of his physical effeminacy or his homosexuality, which is implied by his relationship to the Somonour, who bears "to hym a stif burdoun."[4]

Like the ego, the individual's "persona" is also related to consciousness. Jung's persona should not be confused with the literary definition of persona as the speaker of a poem or as an identity assumed by an author. Jung's persona is "a functional complex that comes into existence for reasons of adaptation or personal convenience, but is by no means identical with the individuality" (Jung 1921, p. 465). In *Two Essays on Analytical Psychology*, Jung further defines this concept:

> Fundamentally the persona is nothing real: it is a compromise between individual and society as to what a man should appear to be. He takes a name, earns a title, represents an office, he is this or that. In a certain sense all this is real, yet in relation to the essential individuality of the person concerned it is only a secondary reality, a product of compromise, in making which others often have a greater share than he. (1953, pp. 167–168)

Later Jung makes the point that individuals often use their personae to impress others or to hide their real natures (ibid., p. 203). The psychological task is to understand the persona is merely a "mask" worn for society and not the true identity. This mask should be variable according to the social milieu in which the individual finds himself. This, as Jacobi observes, requires that the individual be "relatively conscious" of his persona, just as he is conscious of his clothes, which symbolize his persona. If a person identifies too long with his persona, he may be susceptible to "psychic crises and disorders" (1968, pp. 29–30).

In a large measure, the persona is imposed upon an individual by society (and often the family as well). An example is found in Victorian England, where single, middle-class women, for instance, were extremely limited in the "respectable" roles they could play; usually they had a choice between being a teacher or a governess. Becky Sharp, in Thackeray's *Vanity Fair*, begins as a governess. She does not, however, identify with the persona that has been largely imposed upon her. The difficulty in the later nineteenth century of a man's choosing his persona may be seen in Thomas Hardy's *Jude the Obscure* or even in his *The Mayor of Casterbridge*. Jude is never able to fully adjust to society's prescribed role for him; instead of being a stonemason, he would much prefer going to college and becoming a minister. And part, although only part, of Michael Henchard's psychic disintegration comes as a result of the loss of his exalted persona as the mayor of Casterbridge.

The unconscious includes all psychic activity not related directly to the ego. Unlike Freud, who acknowledges only a *personal unconscious*, Jung postulates a *collective unconscious*. The personal unconscious contains "all the acquisitions of personal life, everything forgotten, repressed, subliminally perceived, thought, felt." The collective unconscious has "contents which do not originate in personal acquisitions but in the inherited possibility of psychic functioning in general, i.e., in the motifs and images that can spring up anew anytime, independently of historical tradition or migration" (Jung 1921, p. 485). If the conscious is functioning too one-sidedly (for instance, emphasizing thinking at the expense of feeling), the unconscious will function in a *compensatory* manner, trying to balance the misplaced emphasis. It does this by producing archetypal images in dreams and in fantasies. On a collective scale, the images appear in myths, fairy tales, and formal literature.

Symbols that stand for the unconscious are closely related to the feminine, chthonic world. The earth itself, caves, bodies of water, mazes, and nearly anything that encloses may be considered as symbols not only of the Great Mother, but also of the unconscious. The traditional hero always has to go through what Joseph Campbell calls "the belly of the whale" (1949, pp. 90–94). For the ordinary man, the heroic experience means confronting the unconscious and its symbols in the process of individuation. The symbolism of the confrontation varies: for Jonah, it is a whale; for Theseus, a labyrinth; for Beowulf, the underwater world of Grendel's mother; and for Gawain, both the wasteland through which he passes to find the castle of the Green Knight and the castle itself.

The *process of individuation*, in which the conscious confronts the unconscious, is the central concept of Jung's psychology of the unconscious. Individuation is one of the most important goals of human life and, therefore, of analytical psychology. In *Two Essays on Analytical Psychology*, Jung defines the term: "Individuation means becoming a single, homogeneous being, and, in so far as 'individuality' embraces our innermost, last, and incomparable uniqueness, it also implies becoming one's own self. We could therefore translate individuation as 'coming to selfhood' or 'self-realization' " (1953, p. 182). The true hero-journey for modern man, as W. H. Auden suggests in "The Quest" and "Atlantis," is a phase in the internal search for self-realization or individuation.[5] As Auden suggests in "The Quest," one must admit, if necessary, that one is not heroic in the traditional sense: "And how reliable can any truth be that is got / By observing oneself and then just inserting a Not?" (Auden 1966, p. 185). In order to start the road to individuation, it is necessary to separate the ego from the world of the mother (the womb), and later to distinguish the identity of the individual ego from the collective norm. Individuation does not, however, require separating oneself from and disdaining society; rather, it helps the person to realize his or her own particular uniqueness in his or her own particular environment. "Individuation," Jung says, "leads to a natural esteem for the collective norm," instead of either a separation from or a melting into the norm (1921, p. 449).

The role of the ego is crucial to the process of individuation, for it is through the ego that the symbols of the unconscious become conscious. And, if the conscious successfully assimilates the contents of the unconscious, the change is brought about by the *transcendent function*, "the function which mediates opposites," manifesting itself as a "symbol" (Samuels, Shorter, and Plaut 1986, p. 150).[6] Violet S. de Laszlo calls individuation a "religious experience . . . because it means to live one's own existence creatively in the awareness of its participation in the stream of an eternal becoming" (1958, p. xxix). Indeed, for the many who have lost their faith in traditional religion, individuation can provide a satisfactory alternative (Fordham 1966, p. 76). High levels of individuation can be, and are, achieved by some people without their consciously knowing it, although some Jungians claim that conscious growth is necessary. Others complete the process, or a stage of it, through analysis, but it must be kept in mind that individuation is, strictly speaking, never a finished state of being; rather, it is a continuing process, in fact, a struggle.[7] Finally, it goes without saying that most people never come to self-realization or "wholeness."

The individuation process is divided into two parts. The first part is limited to the first half of life. The goal is adaptation to one's outer environment. As Jacobi puts it, the task is "consolidation of the ego, differentiation of the main function and the dominant attitude type, and development of an appropriate persona" (1968, p. 108). In other words, during the first half of life the tasks are mainly on the level of consciousness as opposed to the unconscious.

Jung's central contributions to the psychology of consciousness are his theories of *psychological types* and the *functions of consciousness*. Basic to this theory of psychological types are the terms *introversion* and *extraversion*, terms which are part of our everyday vocabulary. Few people, however, are aware that Jung coined these terms, and fewer still know his precise definitions of them. In analytical psychology, these terms refer to *attitude types*, and, as Edinger points out, they relate to "innate differences in temperament which cause individuals to perceive and react to life in different fashions" (1968, p. 2). Jung states: "Introversion or extraversion, as a typical attitude, means an essential bias which conditions the whole psychic process, establishes the habitual reactions, and thus determines not only the style of behavior, but also the nature of subjective experience" (1933, p. 86). An introvert turns his libido inward and withdraws from the object, outside of himself, and into the subject, within himself.[8] An extravert, on the other hand, turns his psychic energy (libido) outward: "extraversion is a transfer of interest from subject to object" (Jung 1921, p. 427). Everyone has both introverted and extraverted tendencies, but generally one type is predominant. Usually the one type will look down upon the other: "To the extravert, the introvert is self-centered and withholding of himself. To the introvert, the extravert seems shallow, opportunistic and hypocritical" (Edinger 1968, p. 2).

In addition to the attitude types, there are the four function types (otherwise called functions of consciousness): *thinking, feeling, sensation,* and *intuition*. Jacobi defines thinking as "the function which seeks to apprehend the world and adjust to it by way of thought or cognition, i.e., logical inferences" (1968, p. 12). Feeling should not be confused with the functions of sensation or intuition. Jung defines it as:

> primarily a process that takes place between the ego . . . and a given content, a process, moreover, that imparts to the content a definite *value* in the sense of acceptance or rejection ("like" or "dislike"). . . . [F]eeling is a kind of *judgment*, differing from intellectual judgment in that its aim is not to establish conceptual relations but to set up a subjective criterion of acceptance or rejection. (1921, p. 434)

The two types form opposite poles, and if one type is stronger in the individual, the other is inferior, that is, not as well developed. Both of these types are rational: "both work with evaluations and judgments: thinking evaluates through cognition from the standpoint of 'true-false,' feeling through the emotions from the standpoint of 'pleasant-unpleasant' " (Jacobi 1968, p. 12). The other two types, sensation and intuition, are irrational; they do not evaluate or judge; instead, they perceive.

Each individual tends to use the function that best suits him. This is called the *superior function* while the least suitable function is the *inferior* (Edinger 1968, p. 2; Jung 1968, p. 16). Hardly ever are things so clear-cut as this explanation tends to make them seem because every person has the potential for using all four functions, and that is the ideal goal for wholeness. If the individual develops a second function to almost the same strength as the first, and this is often the case, it is called an *auxiliary function* (Edinger 1968, p. 3).

The sensation type perceives the world through his or her conscious senses, and the intuitive type perceives through his or her unconscious (Jung 1933, p. 91). Just as thinking and feeling are at opposite poles, so are sensation and intuition. All four functions vary in each person according to attitude type. Thus, in a sense, there are eight general types with many variations in between. Jung sums up the four functions in this way: "Sensation establishes what is actually given, thinking enables us to recognize its meaning, feeling tells us its value, and finally intuition points to the possibilities of the whence and whither that lie within the immediate facts" (ibid., p. 93).

Perhaps a few literary examples will help to clarify. At the risk of overgeneralization, one might say that extraversion and introversion have characterized whole literary periods. The Elizabethan era, for instance, was more in the first category, its most popular genre, the drama, being directed toward the object—the audience. The Romantic period is in the second class on the whole, the poet, as in Keats's odes, looking inward to himself. I should note, however, that my use of introversion and extraversion here in connection with literature is slightly different from the way Jung used the terms in 1922 to classify kinds of literary art. In "On the Relation of Analytical Psychology to Poetry," Jung called art "introverted" in which the material used by the artist was completely controlled by his consciousness. In "extraverted" art, "the consciousness of the poet is not identical with the creative process" (Jung 1931a, pp. 73–74). In a later essay, "Psychology and Literature" (1950), Jung elaborated on the two types, renaming the introverted, "psychological," and the extraverted, "visionary," as we have seen.

In this sense, Keats's odes are extraverted. Jung would probably have called most of Pope's work, excluding his translations, introverted (it is hardly "visionary"), but I still think that "extraverted" is more suitable because Pope's libido or psychic energy flows outward.

When it comes to the functions of consciousness, it is harder to make generalizations about literature, for it is hard to assign a function (or even an attitude type, at times) to a great piece of literary art. We can talk, however, about individual characters, and say that George Eliot's Casaubon, in *Middlemarch*, is an introverted-thinking type or that Henry Fielding's Tom Jones is an extraverted-sensation type. In this way we can better understand why a character acts as he does and why others react to him the way they do. We can see, for instance, why Dorothea Brooke, an extraverted-feeling type, feels trapped by her marriage to Casaubon: they are at opposite poles as far as their types are concerned. Tom Jones and Sophia Western, on the other hand, have enough in common, she being an extraverted-feeling type, that they are naturally drawn to each other by their psychological types, as well as by their physical attraction.

Jung concentrated mainly on the second half of life, and on the individuation process, where the job is to look inward to develop one's inner unique personality. Each new level of consciousness, or phase of individuation, that is achieved is characterized by a symbolic *death* and *rebirth*.

As with the quest of the hero, the process of individuation starts with a "call," possibly in the form of an injury to the personality or a mental boredom, like existential dread (von Franz 1964, pp. 166–167). The next step is realization of the *shadow*, then of the *anima* or the *animus*, and finally of the *Self* (ibid., pp. 168–229; Jung 1951, chapters 2–4). I shall discuss each of these archetypal symbols separately. Suffice it to say at this point that, in general, the analysis of literature from the Jungian point of view explores the stages in the process of individuation. Some works, such as the epic, the drama, and the novel, are long enough to portray the success or failure in reaching wholeness; others, including the short lyric, the short play, and the short story, can encompass only part of the process.

The encounter with the shadow is the first major stage in the process of individuation. Although the shadow is an archetype of the collective unconscious, "its nature," Jung writes, "can in large measure be inferred from the contents of the personal unconscious" (1951, p. 8). It is the dark opposite side of ourselves that we usually prefer to hide from others, and often from ourselves. The shadow is always personified by a member of

9.

one's own sex. It is easier to recognize and understand than the anima or the animus because

> with the shadow, we have the advantage of being prepared in some sort by our education, which has always endeavoured to convince people that they are not one-hundred-percent pure gold. So everyone immediately understands what is meant by "shadow," "inferior personality," etc. And if he has forgotten, his memory can easily be refreshed by a Sunday sermon, his wife, or the tax collector. (Ibid., p. 17)

An individual can avoid recognition of the shadow, or its "assimilation" into his "conscious personality," by projection. He may perceive certain of his shadow traits, but he will not fully admit them to himself because the emotion of those traits "appears to lie, beyond all possibility of doubt, in the *other person*" (ibid., p. 9). Shakespeare's Caliban, who fits Jung's definition of the shadow exactly ("the adverse representation of the dark chthonic world" (ibid., p. 34)), projects his own shadow onto Prospero and thus remains oblivious of his true self. Prospero, on the other hand, is psychologically mature, what Jung would call individuated; he has come to terms with his shadow and does not feel threatened by it.[9]

The shadow is not always negative; dark may connote the unknown as well as the menacing. Edinger writes that "in many cases unconscious positive potentialities of the personality reside in the shadow. In such cases we speak of a *positive shadow*" (1968, p. 5). In literature there are many examples of contrasting pairs of the same sex. Often one is "evil" while the other is "good." Such a pair are Fielding's Blifil and Tom Jones. Each may be considered the shadow of the other. Blifil, in particular, has projected his own evil nature. Although Fielding probably would deny that either has the potentialities of the other, psychologically we know that they do. Another case of shadow projection is Oscar Wilde's *The Picture of Dorian Gray* (see Chapter Four). In order to avoid facing it, Gray, whose very name suggests his dark nature, projects his "inferior personality" onto his hidden portrait. The psychological danger of carrying such projection to the extreme is demonstrated by Gray's destruction at the end of the novel. Perhaps the clearest example in literature of the split nature of man is the one Jung himself cites in *Man and His Symbols*: Stevenson's *Dr. Jekyll and Mr. Hyde* (Jung et al. 1964, p. 58).[10]

After recognizing and accommodating the shadow, the next step in the process of individuation is, for a man, the accommodation of the anima; for a woman, it is the accommodation of the animus, which I shall discuss more fully later. The anima is the feminine side of a man's psyche, just as the animus is the masculine side of a woman's psyche. As Jacobi writes in *The Psychology of C. G. Jung*:

> The archetypal figure of the soul-image [i.e., the anima or the animus] always stands for the complementary, contra-sexual part of the psyche, reflecting both our personal rela-tion to it and the individual human experience of the contra-sexual. It represents the image of the other sex that we carry in us as individuals and also as members of the species. (1968, p. 114)

For Jung, the anima is "the personification of the inferior functions which relate a man to the collective unconscious. The collective unconscious as a whole presents itself to a man in feminine form." (He adds that "to a woman it appears in masculine form, and then I call it the *animus*" (Jung 1968, p. 99).)[11]

Jungian psychologist von Franz defines the anima as "a personification of all feminine psychological tendencies in a man's psyche, such as vague feelings and moods, prophetic hunches, receptiveness to the irrational, capacity for personal love, feeling for nature, and — last but not least — his relation to the unconscious" (1964, p. 177). Yet another Jungian, Barbara Hannah, explains the role of the contrasexual image in the individuation process: "The struggle between ego and shadow . . . can seldom or never be solved without the intervention of the following phase, the struggle between the human being and animus or anima, just as the latter can never be solved without the intervention of the Self" (1971, p. 55). The anima and the animus stand, as it were, in the middle of the second half of the individuation process.

The anima and the animus are harder to acknowledge than the shadow, for they are rooted deep in the collective unconscious. The anima is, indeed, as von Franz points out, the "personification of a man's uncon-scious" (1964, p. 178). Furthermore, whether the anima takes a negative or a positive shape in an individual is largely determined by the man's relationship with his mother. Once the parental "imago" has been split off from man's consciousness, the anima assumes the form of a woman. She may be an inner manifestation, as in dreams or fantasies; or she may be projected onto an actual woman. Jung writes that, "she is . . . a very influential factor, and, like the parents, she produces an imago of a rela-tively autonomous nature — not an imago to be split off like that of the parents, but one that has to be kept associated with consciousness" (1953,

p. 198). The psychological danger is disassociating the anima from the consciousness. If a man does not come to terms with the anima, he may not be able to "distinguish himself from her" (ibid., p. 205). When this happens to a married man, his wife may exercise "an illegitimate authority over him" (ibid., p. 208). He runs the risk of becoming overly effeminate and succumbing to the "moods" of his "soul-image" that are buried in his unconscious. Jung says that "the repression of feminine traits and inclinations naturally causes these contrasexual demands to accumulate in the unconscious" (ibid., p. 199). This can be a very real danger, especially since in Western culture, unfortunately, "a man counts it a virtue to repress his feminine traits as much as possible" (ibid.).

As with all archetypal symbols, the anima may have either a negative or a positive influence. Or it may be a mixture of both in any of its manifestations. In *Man and His Symbols*, von Franz succinctly outlines the four stages of the anima as it can be realized in a man:

> The first stage is best symbolized by the figure of Eve, which represents purely instinctual and biological relations. The second can be seen in Faust's Helen: She personifies a romantic and aesthetic level that is, however, still characterized by sexual elements. The third is represented, for instance, by the Virgin Mary — a figure who raises love (*eros*) to the heights of spiritual devotion. The fourth type is symbolized by Sapientia, wisdom transcending even the most holy and the most pure. Of this another symbol is the Shulamite in the Song of Solomon. (1964, p. 185)

Von Franz further points out that modern man seldom reaches the final stage.

What the anima is for a man, the animus is for a woman. Just as the initial image of the anima in a man stems from his mother, so the image of a woman's animus starts in her father. When a woman succumbs to the negative animus, she becomes opinionated instead of reflective; she is not logical. As Jung writes, "the animus is partial to argument, and he can best be seen at work in disputes where both parties know they are right" (1951, p. 15). An animus-possessed woman is concerned with power. When anima and animus meet, the "relationship is always full of 'animosity,' i.e., it is emotional, and hence collective" (ibid., p. 16). Some of the more negative characteristics of the animus are "brutality, recklessness, empty talk, and silent, obstinate, evil ideas" (von Franz 1964, p. 193). On the positive side, "in the same way that the anima gives relationship and relatedness to a man's consciousness, the animus gives woman's consciousness a capacity for reflection, deliberation, and self-knowledge" (Jung 1951, p. 16). Von Franz points out that the animus can also "personify an enterprising spirit, courage, truthfulness, and in the highest form, spiritual profundity" (1964, p. 195).

Like the anima, the animus also has four levels of development. Von Franz lists them:

> He first appears as a personification of mere physical power—for instance, as an athletic champion or "muscle man." In the next stage he possesses initiative and the capacity for planned action. In the third phase, the animus becomes the "word," often appearing as a professor or clergyman. Finally, in his fourth manifestation, the animus is the incarnation of *meaning*. On this highest level he becomes (like the anima) a mediator of the religious experience whereby life acquires new meaning. He gives the woman spiritual firmness, an invisible inner support that compensates for her outer softness. (1964, p. 194)

Just as the anima, according to Jung, represents the "maternal Eros," so the animus "corresponds to the paternal Logos" (Jung 1951, p. 14).

We can see the compensatory power of the animus in D. H. Lawrence's short story, "The Horse Dealer's Daughter." In that story, Mabel Pervin is alienated from the animus; she has no consciousness of her masculine side. She has so given herself over to the feminine that she tries to drown herself in a pond (itself a symbol of the feminine, as well as of the unconscious) in order to join her dead mother. Jack Fergusson, a local doctor, rescues her, and she realizes she loves him. He represents her rational animus, which hitherto she had not encountered. Together they start on the road to psychic wholeness.

Henry James's Isabel Archer, in *The Portrait of a Lady*, on the other hand, is too much possessed by the animus. She rejects two men, Caspar Goodwood and Lord Warburton, who are combinations of the first two animus stages. In order to keep her independence and freedom, she marries a dilettante, Gilbert Osmond, who is himself anima-possessed. The marriage is, predictably, a disaster.

The negative aspect of the animus is also embodied in the dark men who are the subjects of Sylvia Plath's poems, poems such as "Full Fathom Five," "Man in Black," and "Daddy." The failure to come to terms with the animus in such poems also forebodes disaster. There is not much hope of psychic health for the speaker who declares: "Daddy, daddy, you bastard, I'm through" (Plath 1981, p. 224). While it is psychically necessary for a woman to declare her independence from her father, she must also accommodate the animus, the image of which stems from her father.

The culmination — indeed, the goal — of the individuation process is the realization of the Self. Full knowledge of the Self is never reached in life, but various degrees of self-knowledge can be achieved, especially in the second half of life. For Jung, the Self "designates the whole range of psychic phenomena in man. It expresses the unity of the personality as a whole." Since we can never fully know, or be conscious of, the unconscious part of ourselves, "the self is, in part, only *potentially* empirical and is to that extent a *postulate*" (Jung 1921, p. 460). The archetype of the Self, as Edinger notes, "often appears as a process of centering [i.e., balancing] or as a process involving the union of opposites" (1968, p. 7). Thus, as we shall see, the *hieros gamos* and the hermaphrodite are symbols of the Self. Furthermore, what Jung calls a "supraordinate personality" (for example, a hero, king, prophet, or savior) may also symbolize the Self. Geometrical figures such as the mandala stand for the Self, as may many other symbols, including animals, stones, and jewels.

The paradoxes of Keats's "Ode on a Grecian Urn," which Cleanth Brooks has explicated, may be considered as betraying a desire for the wholeness that the Self represents and also the wish for stasis once that wholeness is won. It is questionable, however, whether psychic wholeness is achieved in the poem. The libido, or psychic energy, is frozen, as it were, for the lovers of stanza two will never be able to embrace each other; nor will they ever move any farther apart. But the urge toward unity, or totality, is there in the last stanza with the coupling of the opposites suggested by the "Cold Pastoral!" (which is the urn itself) and the famous line: " 'Beauty is truth, truth beauty.' " The urn itself speaks this line, and the urn itself may be considered a symbol of the Self. As I indicated earlier, there are infinite possibilities for the expression of an archetypal symbol. I would like now to examine some of the symbols of the Self that Jung has discovered. These include: the mandala, the *hieros gamos*, the hermaphrodite, the Wise Old Man and Woman, and the God-image.

Mandala is a Sanskrit word meaning a "circle" (Jung 1969, p. 3). Often it will be squared; that is, it will contain a square, the four points of which usually touch the circumference of the circle. Jung calls the mandala the *"archetype of wholeness,"* and declares: "The 'squaring of the circle' is one of the many archetypal motifs which form the basic patterns of our dreams and fantasies" (ibid., p. 4). Mandalas have appeared throughout history, and they are *"symbols of unity and totality"* (Jung

1951, p. 31). Mandalas are also symbols of order as is shown by the ancient swastika, a symbol which, as Jung points out, was adopted by a people badly in need of order — Germany of the 1930s (Jung 1946, pp. 220–221). In 1918–1919, while drawing his own mandalas, Jung came to realize that his "mandalas were cryptograms concerning the state of the self . . . I acquired through them a living conception of the self." He also came to see that "the mandala is the center. It is the exponent of all paths. It is the path to the center, to individuation" (Jung 1963, p. 196).

When they appear in literature, mandalas can mean a need or desire for wholeness or Selfhood, especially if the mandala is imperfect; or they can symbolize the current psychic state, which may have reached a new stage of self-realization or even the completion of individuation. King Arthur's round table is an obvious mandala, standing for, as Merlin initially intended in Malory's *Morte Darthur*, "the rowndenes signyfyed by right." When it disintegrates, it symbolizes the end of wholeness — the fall of the court of Arthur. Another symbolic mandala is found in the seventeenth-century poem, "The World," by Henry Vaughan, which begins: "I saw Eternity the other night / Like a great *Ring* of pure and endless light." The ring is connected with Christ, who is also a symbol of the Self (Jung 1951, Chapter 5) at the end of the poem: "*This Ring the Bride-groome did for none provide / But for his bride.*" We have here a *hieros gamos*, another symbol of wholeness: Christ, the "Light of the World," married to his bride, the earthly Church; the poem ends with a cluster of three archetypal symbols — the mandala, Christ, and the *hieros gamos* — all standing for psychic wholeness.

The term *hieros gamos* means "sacred wedding" (Jung 1931b, p. 156) and stands for the wholeness achieved by the union of opposites, especially by coming to terms with the contrasexual, the anima in man, the animus in woman. The *coniunctio* signifies essentially the same thing. Of it, Jung says, in *Mysterium Coniunctionis*: "The factors which come together . . . are conceived as opposites, either confronting one another in enmity or attracting one another in love" (1955–1956, p. 3). In alchemy the opposites range from moist/dry to Sol/Luna. In modern literature, as in analytical psychology, the union of the opposites need not be divine in the Christian sense, but it is religious as Jung uses the term. Much of the fiction of D. H. Lawrence ("The Horse Dealer's Daughter" or "The Virgin and the Gipsy," for instance) illustrates the need for the *hieros gamos* in the twentieth century.

The hermaphrodite is closely related in its symbolism to the *hieros gamos*. In a discussion of the hermaphroditism of the divine child, Jung says: "The hermaphrodite means nothing less than a union of the strongest and most striking opposites" (1953, p. 92). Like the *hieros gamos*, the hermaphrodite shows a completeness illustrated by a man's coming to terms with the anima or a woman with the animus, what Jung calls the *syzygy* (1951, p. 11). The syzygy is the *sine qua non* for the achievement of Selfhood; and the hermaphrodite as a symbol of Selfhood is an image of wholeness that itself "consists in the union of the conscious and the unconscious personality" (Jung 1953, p. 94). In Shakespeare's comedies, such as *The Merchant of Venice* or *Twelfth Night*, when the hermaphroditic theme is suggested by women dressed as men, the outcome is always one of wholeness or a return to balance. The marriages with which *Twelfth Night* ends, for instance, symbolize the union of both sexes.[12]

As symbols of the Self, the Wise Old Man and the Wise Old Woman are "supraordinate personalities." They are helpers and guides for the hero or for the common man in his quest for individuation. As Jung says of the masculine image of this archetype, "The old man knows what roads lead to the goal and points them out to the hero" (de Laszlo 1958, p. 76). The Wise Old Man and the Wise Old Woman stand for the highest spiritual wisdom and the wholeness represented by the Self. Sometimes, for older people, the Self may appear as a youth (von Franz 1964, pp. 196–198). Literature is filled with examples of the Wise Old Man in particular, but it has examples of the Wise Old Woman also — Naomi, in the Book of Ruth, for instance. Naomi helps guide Ruth to spiritual renewal in a new land. The sage and mage of King Arthur's court, Merlin, is a symbol of the whole man and an archetypal image of the Wise Old Man (E. Jung and von Franz 1980, p. 348), one especially needed in the Middle Ages and, as I will show in the next chapter, in the nineteenth century as well. Finally, the old man in Chaucer's "The Pardoner's Tale" symbolizes the self-realization that the youthful rioters reject.

I have saved the God-image for last because it is the highest order of supraordinate personalities, and because it is a major concern of literature from the Victorian era to the present. Aniela Jaffé succinctly defines this archetypal image in her glossary for Jung's *Memories, Dreams, Reflections*:

> [The God-image is] derived from the Church Fathers, according to whom the *imago Dei* is imprinted on the human soul. When such an image is spontaneously produced in dreams, fantasies, visions, etc., it is, from the psychological point of view, a symbol of the self . . . of psychic wholeness. (Jung 1963, p. 394)

The God-image is not itself a supernatural being but the image of what might be called the God archetype, as well as the archetype of the Self. Jung believes that there is an innate spiritual dimension in human beings that requires fulfillment before they can be psychically healthy. If a person cannot experience the God-image — a representation of spiritual wholeness — by means of traditional religion, he or she can do it through the process of individuation.

Even a cursory glance at the literature of the last one hundred and fifty years will reveal a need for spiritual gratification. Tennyson in particular reflects this need in the face of nineteenth-century scientific discoveries that seemed so inimical to religious faith. *In Memoriam* begins with a hopeful assertion of faith in the God-image:

> Strong Son of God, immortal Love,
>> Whom we, that have not seen thy face,
>> By faith, and faith alone, embrace,
> Believing where we cannot prove. . . .

Here Christ is the image of God, just as a son often may be considered the image of his father. At the end of his life, the God-image again reveals its power in Tennyson's poem, "Crossing the Bar": "I hope to see my Pilot face to face / When I have crost the bar." All that the speaker of the poem can offer is hope that the self-realization offered by the symbol of the God-image, his "Pilot," is real and will sustain him after death.

In the twentieth century the possibility of a firm hope is even more difficult, as Flannery O'Connor's *Wise Blood* so aptly illustrates. No matter how hard he tries, the novel's protagonist, Hazel Motes, cannot shake the image of God within him. This fact, O'Connor feels, proves his "integrity." To her, "belief in Christ is to some a matter of life and death," but for those who don't understand this fact, "Hazel Motes' integrity lies in his trying with such vigor to get rid of the ragged figure who moves from tree to tree in the back of his mind" (O'Connor 1962, p. 8). The reason the image is so powerful has to do not only with Motes's personal history but also the fact that he is confronted with an archetypal image which stems from deep within the collective unconscious. The need for spiritual fulfillment is rooted deep in our collective experience.

One way of viewing the problem posed by Samuel Beckett's *Waiting for Godot* is that modern man lacks a viable God-image. Nowhere is the difficulty of establishing a firm image of God more clear than in T. S. Eliot's "The Hollow Men": the loss of religious faith and the implicit need for an image of God are suggested by the unfinished Lord's Prayer at the end of the poem. Eliot's later poetry expresses a much closer relationship to and knowledge of the spiritual, indicating that he, as artist, and probably as man, came to realize the God-image.

I have attempted to elucidate Jung's psychology of the conscious and the unconscious and his theory of creativity and to show how these can be used as effective tools in criticizing literature. As I have indicated, I do not feel Jungian criticism is the only kind worth practicing, but I do believe that it can lead to discovery of many hitherto unexplored truths in literature. I hope the succeeding chapters provide some examples of these truths.

Notes

1. The first two realizations of the Self for Tristram are his two periods of happiness with Iseult (in cantos 2 and 6). These are less mature stages in Tristram's process of individuation, the process that leads to full psychic balance.

2. A contemporary example of such a work is William Peter Blatty's *The Exorcist*. Speaking of the film version of this novel, Dr. Thayer Greene, a Jungian analyst, says: "Modern consciousness has become so rationalized . . . that the reaction to this kind of movie is a compensatory upthrust of irrational forces — not necessarily evil" (quoted in *Newsweek*, February 11, 1974, p. 63). I think also that the demon-possessed child in *The Exorcist* represents the collective shadow — an archetypal image of the evil modern society often prefers to ignore. As an aesthetic whole, however, *The Exorcist* is not satisfactory, being, at its worst, blatant sensationalism. Another example from recent popular culture is George Lucas's *Star Wars* trilogy. Joseph Campbell says the following about the first of the three movies: "It asks, Are you going to be a person of heart and humanity — because that's where the life is, from the heart — or are you going to do whatever seems to be required of you by what might be called 'intentional power'? When Ben Kenobi says, 'May the Force be with you,' he's speaking of the power and energy of life, not of programmed political intentions" (Campbell and Moyers 1988, p. 144). Beyond its technical brilliance, the popularity of the trilogy can be explained by its representation of characters, patterns, and themes its audiences respond to instinctually because these characters, patterns, and themes are rooted in the collective unconscious.

3. I capitalize the Self throughout this book in order to distinguish it from the non-Jungian use of the word.

4. For further comment on this relationship, see Ann S. Haskell, "The St. Joce Oath in The Wife of Bath's Prologue," *The Chaucer Review* 1 (1966):86.

5. For a fuller discussion of "Atlantis," see Chapter Seven on Auden.

6. The transcendent function refers to the process wherein the ego creates a synthesis between the conscious and the unconscious, the "real and imaginary, or rational and irrational data" (Samuels, Shorter, and Plaut 1986, p. 150); the ego by creating a new archetypal symbol puts "an end to the division and . . . [forces] the energy of the opposites into a common channel" (Jung 1921, p. 480). The function is complex because it is composed of the other functions. "Transcendent" has nothing to do with metaphysics, but rather means that a new attitude has transpired by means of this function. The transcendent function explains some of the seemingly inexplicable changes in characters in fiction — the new attitude of D. H. Lawrence's horse dealer's daughter (in the story of the same name), for example, after she begins to assimilate the animus. See below for a fuller discussion of this story.

7. In *Psyche and Symbol in Shakespeare*, Alex Aronson points out that for some,

the "fullest and most intense self-realization" can only be found in death (1972, p. 34).

8. For Jung, the unconscious is the origin of the libido: "it [the unconscious] not only contains but is itself the origin of the libido from which the psychic elements flow" (1953, p. 177). The libido is "psychic energy," and the terms "libido" and "energy" are often used by Jung interchangeably (1921, pp. 455–457). Violet S. de Laszlo describes this Freudian term as used by Jung:

> For Jung the concept of *libido* has a different or rather wider meaning than it had for Freud. It comprehends the sum total of the energic life processes, of all the vital forces of which sexuality represents only one area. Jung speaks of libido as an energy value which is able to communicate itself to any field of activity whatsoever, be it power, hunger, hatred, sexuality, or religion, without ever being itself a specific instinct. (1958, p. xxxi)

Fordham explains that the libido is not a force "as such," but a term for "observed phenomena." Furthermore, the libido flows between two contrary poles which Jung generally terms "the opposites." In order for there to be energy, there must be tension between the poles, and the more tension, the more energy (Fordham 1966, pp. 17–18).

A movement that goes forward, meeting the conscious needs, is called *progression*; the opposite movement, backward toward the unconscious and its needs, is *regression*. Both movements are normal and necessary, and mental illness may result if either one is stymied. The opposites have a "regulating function," writes Fordham, "and when one extreme is reached, libido passes over into its opposite." Other opposites besides progression and regression, subject and object, are "consciousness and unconsciousness, extraversion and introversion, thinking and feeling" (Fordham 1966, pp. 18–19).

Jung's concept of the libido supports his basic tenet about psychic health — that it requires balance. This does not mean stasis, but rather a continuing struggle for balance. Just as the body does not remain static, so the psyche is always moving. As one's age changes, so does one's psychic needs. In each "normal" individual, there is ever a conflict or tension between the opposing parts of his or her psyche. Two of these poles are illustrated by Milton's poems, "L'Allegro" and "Il Penseroso," which represent one kind of extraversion and one kind of introversion. Two other common polarities that have troubled civilized man through the years, the physical and the spiritual, have been explored by such diverse seventeenth-century poets as Anne Bradstreet ("The Flesh and the Spirit") and Andrew Marvell ("A Dialogue Between the Soul and the Body"). In a sense, Milton's poems deal with the same polarities. The conflict, reflected in the Mary and Martha episode of the New Testament, is archetypal. The solution to the conflict is the realization that the physical and the spiritual cannot be separated, a fact which modern man, in the process of "losing" his "soul," has failed to recognize.

9. See Aronson (1972, pp. 191–192, 258–259) for a further Jungian interpretation of Caliban and his relationship to Prospero.

10. For an extended Jungian analysis of Stevenson's story, see Hannah, *Striving for Wholeness* (1971, pp. 43–56).

11. In general, "men are predominantly thinking or sensation types while women tend to be feeling or intuitive types, the opposite characteristics (which are latent in everybody) being associated with the contrasexual complex" (Stevens 1982, p. 195). Thus a man's anima would embody the intuition and feeling functions if, indeed, these were inferior in him.

12. Aronson points out, however, that the union achieved in Shakespeare's comedies "is never the result of a mature longing for self-realization. The hero is still in his early manhood, quite unaware of the need to strive towards completeness" (1972, p. 32). Nevertheless, a level of Selfhood is reached that may pave the way for future development.

Works Cited

Abrams, M. H. 1957. *A Glossary of Literary Terms*. New York: Rinehart.

Auden, W. H. 1966. *Collected Shorter Poems: 1927–1957*. New York: Vintage.

Aronson, Alex. 1972. *Psyche and Symbol in Shakespeare*. Bloomington, Ind.: Indiana University Press.

Campbell, Joseph. 1949. *The Hero with a Thousand Faces*. New York: World.

Campbell, Joseph, and Moyers, Bill. 1988. *The Power of Myth*. Betty Sue Flowers, ed. New York: Doubleday.

Crane, Ronald. 1953. *The Languages of Criticism and the Structure of Poetry*. Toronto: University of Toronto Press.

de Laszlo, Violet S., ed. 1958. *Psyche and Symbol: A Selection from the Writings of C. G. Jung*. Garden City, N.Y.: Doubleday Anchor.

Edinger, Edward F. 1968. An outline of analytical psychology. In *Quadrant: Notes on Analytical Psychology*, reprint I. New York: The C. G. Jung Foundation for Analytical Psychology.

Fordham, Frieda. 1966. *An Introduction to Jung's Psychology*. Harmondsworth, England: Penguin.

Frye, Northrop. 1957. *Anatomy of Criticism: Four Essays*. New York: Atheneum.

Hannah, Barbara. 1971. *Striving for Wholeness*. New York: Putnam's.

Haskell, Ann S. 1966. The St. Joce oath in "The Wife of Bath's Prologue." *The Chaucer Review* 1:85–87.

Jacobi, Jolande. 1959. *Complex/Archetype/Symbol in the Psychology of C. G. Jung.* Ralph Manheim, trans. Princeton, N.J.: Princeton University Press.

_____. 1968. *The Psychology of C. G. Jung: An Introduction with Illustrations.* Ralph Manheim, trans. New Haven, Conn.: Yale University Press.

Jacoby, Mario. 1969. The analytical psychology of C. G Jung and the problem of literary evaluation. Maria Pelikan, trans. Joseph Strelka, ed. *Problems of Literary Evaluation.* University Park, Pa.: Pennsylvania State University Press.

Jung, C. G. 1921. *Psychological Types.* CW, vol. 6. Princeton, N.J.: Princeton University Press, 1971.

_____. 1931a. On the relation of analytical psychology to poetry. *CW* 15:65–83. Princeton, N.J.: Princeton University Press, 1966.

_____. 1931b. The structure of the psyche. *CW* 8:139–158. Princeton, N.J.: Princeton University Press, 1960.

_____. 1933. *Modern Man in Search of a Soul.* W. S. Dell and Cary F. Baynes, trans. New York: Harcourt.

_____. 1934a. Sigmund Freud in his historical setting. *CW* 15:33–40. Princeton, N.J.: Princeton University Press, 1966.

_____. 1934b. "Ulysses": a monologue. *CW* 15:109–134. Princeton, N.J.: Princeton University Press, 1966.

_____. 1946. The fight with the shadow. *CW* 10:218–226. Princeton, N.J.: Princeton University Press, 1964.

_____. 1950. Psychology and literature. *CW* 15:84–105. Princeton, N.J.: Princeton University Press, 1966.

_____. 1951. *Aion. CW*, vol. 9ii. Princeton, N.J.: Princeton University Press, 1959.

_____. 1953. *Two Essays on Analytical Psychology.* R. F. C. Hull, trans. New York: World.

_____. 1955–1956. *Mysterium Coniunctionis. CW*, vol. 14. Princeton, N.J.: Princeton University Press, 1963.

_____. 1963. *Memories, Dreams, Reflections.* Richard and Clara Winston, trans. Aniela Jaffé, ed. New York: Vintage.

_____. 1968. *Analytical Psychology, Its Theory and Practice: The Tavistock Lectures.* New York: Vintage.

_____. 1969. *Mandala Symbolism.* R. F. C. Hull, trans. Princeton, N.J.: Princeton University Press.

Jung, C. G. et al. 1964. *Man and His Symbols.* Garden City, N.Y.: Doubleday.

Jung, C. G., and Kerényi, C. 1963. *Essays on a Science of Mythology: The*

Myth of the Divine Child and the Mysteries of Eleusis. R. F. C. Hull, trans. Princeton, N.J.: Princeton University Press.

Jung, Emma, and von Franz, Marie-Louise. 1980. *The Grail Legend*. Andrea Dykes, trans. 2nd ed. Boston: Sigo.

Maynadier, Howard. 1907. *The Arthur of the English Poets*. Boston: Houghton.

O'Connor, Flannery. 1962. *Three: Wise Blood, A Good Man Is Hard to Find, The Violent Bear It Away*. New York: Signet.

Philipson, Morris. 1963. *Outline of a Jungian Aesthetics*. Evanston, Ill.: Northwestern University Press.

Plath, Sylvia. 1981. *The Collected Poems*. Ted Hughes, ed. New York: Harper.

Samuels, Andrew; Shorter, Bani; and Plaut, Fred. 1986. *A Critical Dictionary of Jungian Analysis*. London: Routledge.

Stevens, Anthony. 1982. *Archetypes: A Natural History of the Self*. New York: Quill.

von Franz, Marie-Louise. 1964. The process of individuation. In *Man and His Symbols*, C. G. Jung, ed. Garden City, N.Y.: Doubleday.

Wellek, René. 1961. The main trends of twentieth-century criticism. *The Yale Review* 51:102–118.

Chapter Two

The Archetypal Wise Old Man: Merlin in Nineteenth-Century British Literature*

Yea, heart in heart is molten, hers and his,
Into the world's heart and the soul that is
Beyond or sense or vision. . . .

Swinburne, *Tristram of Lyonesse*

Except perhaps for Tristram and Iseult, Merlin more than any other Arthurian figure has retained a separate identity. First named in Geoffrey of Monmouth's *Historia Regum Britanniae* (1135–1147), he was later portrayed by Geoffrey in his *Vita Merlini* (1148–1151) as a South Wales king and prophet. Like such predecessors as Jeremiah and Tiresias, Merlin's initial appearance came during a time of widespread belief in the supernatural. As a literary figure, Merlin benefited from the continuing high esteem for myth and legend held by medieval and early English Renaissance writers.

Around the start of the seventeenth century, however, literary interest in Arthurian legend began to wane. Merlin survived as a viable figure mainly because his prophecies were used to support Tudor and Stuart claims to the throne. Jonson, Milton, and Dryden all showed interest in Arthurian legend, yet none translated that interest into his best work. Merlin became an object of parody or a tool of satire and farce. From approximately 1644 to 1832 his name was used to add authority to numerous astrological works. Not until William Blake was Merlin again treated seriously by a major poet. Eventually other nineteenth-century British authors, major and minor, restored Merlin to his position as the British seer par excellence. Although literal belief in him was unlikely, he compen-

*Portions of this chapter were first published as "Merlin in Victorian Poetry: A Jungian Analysis" in *The Victorian Newsletter*, © 1987, Western Kentucky University, Bowling Green, Kentucky 42101. Reprinted with permission.

sated, in a Jungian sense, for contemporary doubts about the supernatural, as well as for Victorian prudishness. As the archetypal Wise Old Man, he symbolized the whole person — the Self. The story of Merlin's enchantment and imprisonment by a woman especially interested Victorian writers, and whether they treated Merlin's fate as positive or negative suggests how comfortable the major poets were with the psychic tensions of the age.

Although Merlin is not prominent in Blake, Blake takes him seriously. The earliest indication that Merlin's literary reputation is rising is a little poem labeled "Merlin's Prophecy" (c. 1791–1792) (Damon 1965, p. 270):

> The harvest shall flourish in wintry weather,
> When two virginities meet together.
>
> The king and the priest must be tied in a tether
> Before two virgins can meet together.
>
> *(Blake 1971, pp. 160–161)*

The poem, as W. H. Stevenson notes, is in the tradition of the "cryptic sayings" of Merlin's prophecies in Geoffrey's *Historia* (Blake 1971, pp. 160–161); but Blake's little verse adds little else to Merlin as a literary or archetypal figure.

In *Jerusalem, the Emanation of the Great Albion* (1818–1820), however, Blake does make his own use of Merlin. Indeed, as Northrup Frye points out, when Blake uses Merlin's name, it need not "depend for [its] meaning on one's memory of . . . Malory" (Frye 1947, p. 120). For Blake uses Merlin in his own special symbolic system. In *Jerusalem*, as S. Foster Damon shows, Merlin stands for the "immortal Imagination of the Vegetative [that is, the mortal] Man" (Damon 1965, p. 270). Damon explains that Merlin also represents the "enslaved Imagination" and with "Arthur (the enslaved Reason), and Bladud (the enslaved Body) [he] form[s] a triad" (ibid., p. 30). In Geoffrey's *Historia*, Bladud is the tenth king of Britain, the son of Leil and the father of Lear, and, like Merlin, he is a necromancer. Both Merlin and Arthur succumb to what Blake terms the "female will," or what Jung would call the negative anima. Overall, however, Merlin is not especially significant in Blake's poetry.

Referring to Merlin's appearance in the Middle Ages, Emma Jung and Marie-Louise von Franz express surprise at the fact that a mere "literary creation . . .should suddenly have achieved tremendous fame and been responsible for such a vast amount of literature." When such a thing happens, they go on, "it is obvious, from the psychological point of view, that it is a case of the breakthrough of an archetypal image which represents an intensively constellated psychic content" (E. Jung and von Franz 1980, pp. 349–350).

In nineteenth-century Britain we see a similar breakthrough with the reemergence of not only Merlin but the whole Arthurian legend. Contributing to this reemergence, for example, we see two relatively minor romantic poets, John Leyden (1775–1811) and Reginald Heber (1783–1825), continuing the trend, started by Blake, of reinvesting Merlin with literary dignity, reflecting thus the new interest in myth and the supernatural that the great romantic poets were showing. Leyden's *Scenes of Infancy: Descriptive of Teviotdale* (1803) alludes to the Merlin we find in Geoffrey's *Vita Merlini*. Leyden recalls a rather melancholy Merlin sitting under the "apple blossoms" and prophesying that:

> Once more, begirt with many a martial peer,
> Victorious Arthur shall his standard rear,
> In ancient pomp his mailed bands display. . . .
>
> *(pp. 6–7)*

In a few decades, Victorian poets will fulfill this prophecy.

The Spenserian stanzas of Heber's "Morte D'arthur: A Fragment" are indebted to the traditional sources: Geoffrey, Robert de Boron, and Malory. The work is filled with cliches, such as "vale of tears" and "wistful eyes" (Heber 1845, p. 147). But the picture of Merlin is authentic. He is "swart" with "raven hair / Hung loose and long in many a tangled fold." Appearing as a figure from the past, Merlin has "large eyeballs, with [an] unearthly stare." Clearly, this Merlin is the dual-natured son of a devil and a saintly maid we find in the medieval texts. Yet despite this and another rather quixotic treatment that has Merlin chasing a woman named Gwendolen ("Fragments on the Masque of Gwendolen"), neither Leyden nor Heber achieved the kind of "tremendous fame" for Merlin to which Emma Jung and von Franz refer.

The same is true for the innovative creations of Sir Walter Scott and William Wordsworth. In 1813 Scott used Merlin in *The Bridal of Triermain*. As in Ben Jonson's masque, *The Speeches at Prince Henry's Barriers* (1610), Merlin rises from his earthly grave, this time to intervene in a romantic plot. Called the "Wizard Prophet," Merlin angrily tells Gyneth, who has mercilessly watched a number of knights die vying for her favor, that she is to sleep until a knight awakens her. And sleep she does for five hundred years, until awakened by Sir Roland de Vaux, the Baron of Trier-main (Scott 1904, pp. 567–582).

Like Scott, Wordsworth exhibited little more than a passing interest in Arthurian legend. Merlin appears in his rather insignificant poem, "The Egyptian Maid, or, The Romance of the Water Lily" (1835). The Egyptian maid is shipwrecked by a storm Merlin has whimsically raised. She had been on her way to "Caerleon" to marry a knight of the Round Table. Nina, the "Lady of the Lake," has Merlin take the maid to Arthur's court, where she ends up marrying, of all knights, Sir Galahad. The poem disap-points. Wordsworth has invented its particulars, but he fails to provide Merlin with adequate motivation for his actions. Margaret Reid, in *The Arthurian Legend*, aptly comments that Wordsworth does not "penetrate deeply into the heart of legend to find its symbolic and cosmic meaning" (1938, p. 78). Wordsworth's attempt to add to the already immense canon of Arthurian material remains little more than a sentimental love story. From the Jungian point of view, the era was not yet in need of the great compensatory power the Arthurian archetypes, Merlin in particular, would provide.

Such a need arose during the Victorian period, when doubts about the supernatural became widespread and Arthurian legend once again enjoyed a reputation based upon artistic interest as opposed to historical, political, astrological, or satiric interest. In the work of Tennyson and Swinburne, treatments of the legend became what Jung terms visionary, work "that derives its existence from the hinterland of man's mind, as if it had emerged from the abyss of prehuman ages, or from a superhuman world of contrasting light and darkness" (Jung 1950a, pp. 89–90). In other words, work that comes from the collective unconscious and thus has more than a merely personal meaning. Such work compensates for contempo-rary psychic imbalance, addressing, either by negative or positive example, the need for psychic wholeness, what Jung terms individuation.[1]

Matthew Arnold's treatment of Merlin, unlike those by Tennyson and Swinburne, falls into the psychological mode, a work drawn from man's conscious life. In psychological poems there is no "obscurity . . . for they fully explain themselves in their own terms" (Jung 1950a, p. 89). Arnold uses Merlin briefly in his *Tristram and Iseult* (1852). The injured Iseult of Brittany tells her children the story of Merlin's enchantment by Vivian, "that false fay, his [Merlin's] friend, / On her white palfrey." Arnold fol-lows the Vulgate *Merlin*, except that the unhappy Iseult (who "seems one dying in a mask of youth,") gives Vivian the same motives, and in the same words, as Malory's Nymue:

> And in that daisied circle, as men say,
> Is Merlin prisoner till the judgment-day;
> But she herself whither she will can rove —
> For she was *passing weary* of his love.
>
> (Arnold 1950, pp. 147–156, italics mine)

Iseult no doubt identifies herself with Merlin, who has also been betrayed in love. But Arnold adds little to the legend, and his version appeals more to the conscious than to the unconscious mind.

Elsewhere I have maintained that Algernon Charles Swinburne's best poem is *Tristram of Lyonesse* (1882). It is also the most psychologically satisfying of Swinburne's poems because in it both Tristram and Iseult achieve psychic wholeness or "the archetypal Self" (Snider 1977, p. 371). In the same poem Merlin, through union with the anima (symbolized by Nimue), achieves a wholeness emblematic of the wholeness Tristram achieves with Iseult. The poem as a whole is visionary because it compensated for contemporary psychic imbalance, most obvious in Victorian attitudes toward sex. *The Saturday Review*, for example, objected to the "low intrigue" in the poem; and *The Spectator* complained that Swinburne "paints the sensual appetite with a redundancy and excess that excite disgust" (quoted in Hyder 1933, pp. 196–197).

As in Heber's "Morte D'arthur: A Fragment," Merlin appears in Swinburne's *Tristram* as a figure from the past. Tristram and his lover, Iseult of Ireland, are reminiscing about Camelot's past, and Iseult brings up the story of Merlin, the "great good wizard," and Nimue. Both Tristram and Iseult recount how Merlin "takes his strange rest at heart of slumberland . . . in green Broceliande" (Swinburne 1904, p. 106). As Reid points out, Swinburne uses this tale "to give expression to his own pantheistic philosophy" (Reid 1938, p. 80). Merlin's fate is, therefore, a "guerdon gentler far than all men's fate," for Merlin has the comfort of nature and the four seasons (Swinburne 1904, pp. 106–107).[2] Yet Merlin symbolizes something far more complex than Swinburne intended: with Nimue he symbolizes a psychic whole, an individuated person. Just as Tristram and Iseult together form a psychic union, so do Merlin and Nimue:

Yea, heart in heart is molten, hers and his,
Into the world's heart and the soul that is
Beyond or sense or vision; and their breath
Stirs the soft springs of deathless life and death,
Death that bears life, and change that brings forth seed
Of life to death and death to life indeed,
As blood recircling through the unsounded veins
Of earth and heaven with all their joys and pains.

(Ibid., pp. 107–108)

When Tristram himself is about to die, he recalls again the story of Merlin, who "with soft live breath / Takes always all the deep delight of death, / Through love's gift of a woman . . ." (ibid., p. 153). Although he does not know it, Tristram himself will share the same fate with his lover, Iseult.

Only Swinburne among Victorian poets makes the story of Merlin's enchantment by a woman entirely positive, as well he should, for on the psychological level Nimue is the feminine in Merlin's psyche. As Jung puts it, referring to a different story, "the hero has been wafted out of the profane world through his encounter with the anima, like Merlin by his fairy . . . he is like one caught in a marvellous dream, viewing the world through a veil of mist" (1948, p. 245). Heinrich Zimmer (1957) in this century also views Merlin's enchantment positively: "Merlin withdraws . . . into the power that is himself. It only looks as though he had succumbed to it" (p. 197).

Although in *Tristram of Lyonesse* Swinburne concentrates on the one aspect of Merlin's story, Swinburne's *The Tale of Balen* (1896) presents the traditional prophet-adviser, who helps Arthur, as well as Balen and Balan. Merlin is not prominent in either poem, yet he remains a compensatory figure who, in the words of Emma Jung and von Franz, "holds open the approaches to the divine-animal substrata of the psyche" (1980, p. 366). Collectively, Victorian society had become too one-sided, gravitating toward the secular versus the spiritual. Archetypal figures such as Merlin helped balance this one-sidedness, even though no major poet grappled with the medieval story of his being conceived by a devil and a saintly woman. (Tennyson's Merlin merely says, "Envy call[ed] me Devil's son" (1965, p. 360.)

The ways Alfred, Lord Tennyson treats Merlin — at least his early treatments — are good examples of Victorian one-sidedness. Tennyson not only skirts the issue of Merlin's birth, he also skirts the issue of Arthur's conception and birth. Merlin clearly played an important part in Arthur's youth, but Arthur's birth is kept a secret in "The Coming of Arthur" (1869), the first of the *Idylls of the King* as finally arranged (Tennyson 1965, p. 290). Merlin is still "the wise man that ever served / King Uther thro' his magic art" (ibid., p. 290), but he is robbed of the shapeshifting magic he used in the medieval versions of Arthur's conception. Changing the tale to fit Victorian morality, Tennyson makes Arthur a virtuous paragon, like Prince Albert, to whom the *Idylls* are dedicated.

In "Merlin and Vivien," Tennyson draws on Malory, as he did in "The Coming of Arthur," but he changes and broadens the tale significantly.[3] "Merlin and Vivien" was written in 1856 and is the first idyll as such of the *Idylls of the King* that Tennyson wrote (Baum 1948, p. 178). The poem was made available to the public, after an 1857 private printing, in 1859, along with three other idylls: "Enid," "Elaine," and "Guinevere" (Marshall 1963, pp. 136–137). Paull F. Baum comments on the contemporary reception given to "Merlin and Vivien":

> [Benjamin] Jowett liked it best and called it "the naughty one"; and there can be little doubt that Tennyson's poetical handling of the seduction scene gave satisfaction to many other readers. Victorian reticence had here successfully, for a moment, raised the veil. (1948, p. 178)

Tennyson's picture of the licentious Vivien must have had a great unconscious, compensatory appeal to a people who counted it a virtue to repress their sensual, "evil" urges. Had the seduction ended positively, as in Swinburne's version, the reaction might not have been so warm, although the unconscious attraction would have been similar. The fact that all three major poets—Arnold, Swinburne, and Tennyson—chose to focus on Merlin's seduction demonstrates the collective appeal of the story. Despite Merlin's reputation as a wise magician, he also is subject to the wiles of the flesh.

Vivien is usually considered entirely evil (Marshall (1963) says she is "represented as the non-repentant evil woman" (p. 141)), but Douglas W. Cooper rightfully qualifies this judgment:

> True, Tennyson's pen has drawn her in acid. But it has also shown her as a kind of failure. She is unfulfilled, love frustrate. . . . Further, he pictures her physicality . . . as somehow a needed opposite tò Merlin. . . . Together they almost seem to form a mute whole, the one complementing the other. (1966, p. 109)

FIGURE 1
The Beguiling of Merlin (1874), by Edward Burne-Jones

The topic of Merlin's seduction by a woman interested Victorian visual artists, just as it interested Victorian poets. (See Aubrey Beardsley's illustration of the same topic for *Le Morte Darthur*, 1893–94.) This interest on the part of the visual artists further demonstrates the collective appeal of this aspect of Merlin's story.

Cooper writes from a Jungian perspective, and clearly the problem Merlin — and all of Camelot — faces is how to accommodate the contrasexual in all its negative and positive aspects. Merlin and Vivien should have made a whole, as they do in Swinburne. Because they do not, the idyll ends with defeat. Trapped inside the oak tree, Merlin "lay as dead, / And lost to life and use and name and fame" (Tennyson 1965, p. 368).

Tennyson characterizes the mage of Arthur's court as "the most famous man of all those times, / Merlin, who knew the range of all their arts, / Had built the King his havens, ships, and halls, / Was also Bard, and knew the starry heavens; / The people called him Wizard" (ibid., p. 356). Merlin in the *Idylls of the King* is, then, as I have indicated, much the same Merlin found in *Le Morte Darthur*. But unlike Malory, who has Merlin pursuing Nymue, Tennyson makes Vivien the temptress — the negative anima — who eventually ensnares Merlin. When this happens, Merlin is in a very real sense anima-possessed. And Vivien fits Jung's description of the anima in possession of a man: she is "fickle, capricious, moody, uncontrolled and emotional . . . gifted with daemonic intuitions, ruthless, malicious, untruthful, bitchy, double-faced, and mystical" (Jung 1950b, p. 124).

After Vivien initially beguiles him, Merlin "at times / Would flatter his own wish in age for love, / And half believe her true" (Tennyson 1965, p. 356). Then a "great melancholy" falls upon him, and he crosses the English Channel to enter the "wild woods of Broceliande." Symbolically, he is in the realm of the unconscious. Vivien follows him, and there in the forest she successfully subdues him. That she is indeed a temptress Tennyson leaves no doubt. She is described as snakelike, and Merlin himself alludes to the Edenic myth, further evidence that we are dealing here with archetypal issues, with the problem of opposites. When Vivien asks to be taught the charm which "so taught will charm us both to rest" (ibid., p. 358), he says it was a mistake to have mentioned the charm to her:

> "Too much I trusted when I told you that
> And stirr'd this vice in you which ruin'd man
> Thro' woman the first hour. . . ."

> (Ibid., p. 359)

The drama here is nothing less than a reenactment of the primal split, and as such it mirrors the split in the Victorian psyche. Nowhere else does Vivien appear so vicious as she does in "Merlin and Vivien." Part of her motivation is that both her parents died in the war against Arthur. But another part is that, as Cooper suggests, she is frustrated in love. On a deeper level, however, Tennyson unconsciously reflects the frustrations of his age.

Vivien pursues her goal ruthlessly, using all the traditional feminine weapons, including a sharp and a soft tongue and tears. She sings a song, the message of which is " 'trust me not at all or all in all,' " and Merlin "half believed her true, / So tender was her voice, so fair her face, / So sweetly gleam'd her eyes behind her tears . . ." (ibid., p. 359). But it takes a storm finally to make her plans work. She declares that if she has "schemed against thy peace . . . May yon just heaven, that darkens o'er me, send / One flash, that, missing all things else, may make / My scheming brain a cinder, if I lie" (ibid., p. 367). Heaven immediately sends such a flash which sends her clinging to Merlin, swearing her love to him. Here is an example of what Jung calls synchronicity, "the simultaneous occurrence of two meaningfully but not causally connected events" (Jung 1952a, p. 441).[4] The incident is Merlin's last warning; wearily, not unlike Malory's Nymue, he succumbs and is imprisoned in the hollow oak. Ironically, the oak tree symbolizes, according to J. E. Cirlot, "strength and long life" (1962, p. 227). The tree itself, according to Jung, has a "bisexual character" (1952b, p. 221); so that had there been real love between Merlin and Vivien the denouement might have been positive, a successful joining of opposites as in Swinburne's version of the tale. Tennyson's purpose, however, is different. His is a cautionary tale, thus perhaps all the more attractive to his Victorian readers. Tennyson mirrors more than he compensates for the contemporary psychic split.

Merlin remained attractive to Tennyson throughout his life. In 1852 he had used Merlin as a pen name when he contributed verses to *The Examiner* (Luce 1895, p. 424). Toward the end of his life, after a very serious illness, Tennyson wrote "Merlin and the Gleam" (1889), about which the poet's son, Hallam, writes:

> For those who cared to know about his literary history he wrote "Merlin and the Gleam." From his boyhood he had felt the magic of Merlin—that spirit of poetry—which bade him know his power and follow throughout his work a pure and high ideal, with a simple and single devotedness and a desire to ennoble the life of the world, and which helped him through doubts and difficulties to "endure as seeing him who is invisible." (Tennyson 1897, vol. 1, p. xii)

Later Hallam tells us his father said that the Gleam " 'signifies in my poem the higher poetic imagination' " (ibid., vol. 2, p. 366).

Tennyson, then, identified himself with Merlin throughout his life, choosing the ancient British bard and seer as the subject of the poem that recounts his own literary career. Tennyson's identification with Merlin is not at all surprising from the psychological perspective. As one of the Victorian prophet figures, Tennyson had a real life role not unlike Merlin's role during the Middle Ages. Zimmer has written that Merlin symbolizes "the magician as teacher and guide of souls. He is comparable . . . to the *guru*" (1957, p. 181). The same could be written about Tennyson, the great Poet Laureate. The irony is, of course, he did indeed have those "doubts and difficulties" his son refers to — all the more reason he should be drawn to Merlin, an archetypal symbol of the Self, the wizard who set up the Round Table, itself a symbol of wholeness (see E. Jung and von Franz 1980, pp. 373, 399). "Merlin and the Gleam" shows Tennyson's growth as a poet. No longer mirroring the contemporary failure to join psychic opposites, he held up a symbol of the individuated Self, quite a different Merlin from the one in the *Idylls*.

In this final commemorative poem Tennyson follows precisely the rhythms of some old Welsh poems (Haight 1947, p. 558). "Merlin and the Gleam" is thus a link to the past and a looking forward to the "boundless Ocean" (Tennyson 1965, p. 808). The speaker addresses a young mariner:

> O young Mariner,
> You from the haven
> Under the sea-cliff,
> You that are watching
> The gray Magician
> With eyes of wonder,
> *I* am Merlin,
> And *I* am dying,
> *I* am Merlin
> Who follow The Gleam.

The poet then retells his career, albeit not exactly chronologically, ending by exhorting the young mariner to:

> Call your companions,
> Launch your vessel,
> And crowd your canvas,

> And, ere it vanishes
> Over the margin,
> After it, follow it,
> Follow The Gleam.

The penultimate stanza ends:

> There on the border
> Of boundless Ocean,
> And all but in Heaven
> Hovers The Gleam.

About this passage, Jerome H. Buckley comments with insight:

> Like "the great deep" in the *Idylls*, the "boundless Ocean" is
> thus both source and destination, the unknown sea from
> which the singer has come and to which he now returns, and
> all the while the eternity that encompasses the island of time
> across which he has traveled. (1960, p. 242)

It is a journey to completion of the Self. As the final stanza shows, the
speaker exhorts the young mariner to follow the same course — an archetypal
journey from and back to the maternal sea, symbol of the unconscious,
where all opposites are ultimately joined. Whether Tennyson personally
achieved individuation is beside the point: publicly he had assumed the role
of the Wise Old Man (as in Jung's definition, "the personification of meaning and spirit" (1952b, p. 332)); and as I have indicated it is no wonder he
identified with Merlin, the Wise Old Man of Arthur's court.

Tennyson identified the Gleam with Nymue or Vivien (Tennyson
1897, vol. 2, p. 366), but obviously not the Vivien he created in the *Idylls*
(see Haight 1947, pp. 559–560). If, however, the Gleam represents the
"higher poetic imagination," then it must encompass both good and evil.
As we have seen, Vivien is evil, although not entirely so. Tennyson's Gleam
is pure, yet it too encounters the "shadow" of stanza seven, where Tennyson recalls Arthur Hallam's death, which inspired the highest poetic
achievement. So out of evil comes the good: "No longer a shadow, / But
clothed with The Gleam" (lines 19–20). If Tennyson is a great poet, an
embodiment himself of the archetypal Wise Old Man, it is in part because
he grappled with the questions of good versus evil, faith versus doubt, and
came to his own rather tentative conclusion: "I hope to see my Pilot face to
face" ("Crossing the Bar," Tennyson 1965, p. 831). That Tennyson should
recount his literary career by identifying himself with Merlin, the son of a

devil and a virgin, is ultimately quite appropriate. Symbolically, the opposites have been united, at least for Tennyson's vast public.

As the nineteenth century became increasingly secular, serious writers, as well as visual artists, turned for their inspiration to the supernatural, reviving interest in Merlin and Arthurian legend, an interest that has continued throughout the twentieth century (see Spivack 1978). Merlin's legacy, as Emma Jung and von Franz write, "is a symbol of the Self . . . [yet] it is only now that those premonitory intimations of the unconscious which are incarnated in the figure of Merlin—namely the task of the realization of the Self—are appearing, to penetrate into the consciousness of our own age" (1980, p. 399). If that is true, the roots of contemporary interest in Merlin and Arthurian legend are grounded in the nineteenth century, and in the *Idylls of the King* especially, just as the roots of Tennyson's (and Arnold's and Swinburne's) work extend back to the Middle Ages in the work of Thomas Malory, Robert de Boron, and Geoffrey of Monmouth.

Notes

1. John Veitch (1820–1894), an obscure poet and professor of logic and rhetoric at the University of Glasgow, best known for his book, *The History and Poetry of the Scottish Border: Their Main Features and Relations* (1878), wrote about Merlin in that book and in *Merlin and Other Poems* (1889). Veitch's pantheistic and rather pedantic work lacked wide appeal and is, both from literary and psychological points of view, of little interest.

2. More recently, David G. Riede (1978) has called *Tristram* "a myth of the creative poet" (p. 191). Recognizing that Swinburne "confronted the crucial problems of the late nineteenth century as directly as any of his contemporaries," Riede, referring to *Tristram*, says "Swinburne's final poetic creed, though hopeful, is no facile optimism but a call for unblinking acceptance of death and pain and continual strife to live intensely and create continually" (ibid., pp. 217, 213). Earlier in the nineteenth century, John Keats had similarly accepted the pain he so often found mixed with sensual pleasure. When, in "The Eve of St. Agnes" (1819), he alludes to Merlin ("Never on such a night have lovers met, / Since Merlin paid his Demon all the monstrous debt"), it is in the context of Porphyro's wish to see Madeline while "pale enchantment held her sleepy-eyed." He hopes to "win perhaps that night a peerless bride," and, of course, he does (Keats 1959, p. 189). That Keats, unlike Swinburne, apparently sees Merlin's enchantment as negative is therefore ironic.

3. Haight (1947) convincingly asserts, however, that "the version . . . closest to Tennyson's idyll is found in the Vulgate *Merlin*," which Tennyson could have read in Robert Southey's notes to his 1817 edition of Malory (pp. 551–552).

4. Synchronicity is related to what is sometimes called extrasensory perception (ESP). What usually happens is that a conscious or unconscious content appears which is followed by a similar content in the external world — as, for example, when a person dreams that he will see an old friend and this actually happens soon afterwards. Synchronicity can be applied to literature because it is "a modern differentiation of the obsolete concept [sic] of correspondence, sympathy, and harmony" (Jung 1952a, p. 531), all of which form a part of the work of certain writers from earlier periods, the sixteenth and seventeenth centuries in particular. Synchronicity also may help to explain what Ruskin termed the "pathetic fallacy." That is, Jung's idea may suggest how psychic happenings can correspond to natural events in literature — how, for instance, when, in Hawthorne's *The Scarlet Letter*, Hester Prynne and Pearl are in the forest, the sun seems to prefer to shine only on Pearl.

Works Cited

Arnold, Matthew. 1950. *The Poetical Works of Matthew Arnold*, C. B. Tinker and H. F. Lowry, eds. London: Oxford University Press.

Baum, Paull F. 1948. *Tennyson Sixty Years After*. Chapel Hill, N.C.: University of North Carolina Press.

Blake, William. 1971. *The Poems of William Blake*. W. H. Stevenson, ed. Text by David V. Erdman. London: Longman.

Buckley, Jerome H. 1960. *Tennyson: The Growth of a Poet*. Boston: Houghton Mifflin.

Cirlot, J. E. 1962. *A Dictionary of Symbols*. Jack Sage, trans. New York: Philosophical Library.

Cooper, Douglas W. 1966. Tennyson's *Idylls*: a mythography of the self. Dissertation. University of Missouri.

Damon, S. Foster. 1965. *A Blake Dictionary: The Ideas and Symbols of William Blake*. Providence, R.I.: Brown University Press.

Frye, Northrup. 1947. *Fearful Symmetry: A Study of William Blake*. Princeton, N.J.: Princeton University Press.

Geoffrey of Monmouth. 1912. *Histories of the Kings of Britain*. Sebastian Evans, trans. London: J. M. Dent.

_____. 1925. *The Vita Merlini*. John Jay Perry, trans. and ed. *University of Illinois Studies in Language and Literature* 10 (1925).

Haight, Gordon. 1947. Tennyson's Merlin. *Studies in Philology* 44:549–566.

Heber, Reginald. 1845. *The Poetical Works of Reginald Heber*. London.

Hyder, Clyde Kenneth. 1933. *Swinburne's Literary Career and Fame*. Durham, N.C.: Duke University Press.

Jonson, Ben. 1969. *Ben Jonson: The Complete Masques*. Stephen Orgel, ed. New Haven, Conn.: Yale University Press.

Jung, C. G. 1948. The phenomenology of the spirit in fairytales. *CW* 9i:207–254. Princeton, N.J.: Princeton University Press, 1959.

_____. 1950a. Psychology and literature. *CW* 15:84–105. Princeton, N.J.: Princeton University Press, 1966.

_____. 1950b. Concerning rebirth. *CW* 9i:113–149. Princeton, N.J.: Princeton University Press, 1959.

_____. 1952a. Synchronicity: an acausal connecting principle. *CW* 8:417–519. Princeton, N.J.: Princeton University Press, 1960.

_____. 1952b. *Symbols of Transformation. CW*, vol. 5. Princeton, N.J.: Princeton University Press, 1956.

Jung, Emma, and von Franz, Marie-Louise. 1980. *The Grail Legend*. Andrea Dykes, trans. 2nd ed. Boston: Sigo.

Keats, John. 1959. *Selected Poems and Letters*. Douglas Bush, ed. Boston: Houghton Mifflin.

Leydon, John. 1803. *Scenes of Infancy: Descriptive of Teviotdale*. Edinburgh.

Luce, Morton. 1895. *A Handbook to the Works of Alfred Lord Tennyson*. London.

Marshall, George O., Jr. 1963. *A Tennyson Handbook*. New York: Twayne.

Reid, Margaret J. C. 1938. *The Arthurian Legend, Comparison of Treatment in Modern and Medieval Literature: A Study in the Literary Value of Myth and Legend*. Edinburgh: Oliver and Boyd.

Riede, David G. 1978. *Swinburne: A Study of Romantic Mythmaking*. Charlottesville, Va.: University Press of Virginia.

Scott, Sir Walter. 1904. *The Poetical Works of Sir Walter Scott*. J. Logie Robertson, ed. London: Oxford University Press.

Snider, Clifton. 1977. The archetypal self in Swinburne's *Tristram of Lyonesse*. *Psychocultural Review* 1:371–390.

Spivack, Charlotte. 1978. Merlin redivivus: the celtic wizard in modern literature. *The Centennial Review* 22:164–179.

Swinburne, Algernon Charles. 1904. *The Poems of Algernon Charles Swinburne*, vol. 4. New York: Harper.

Tennyson, Alfred Lord. 1965. *Tennyson: Poems and Plays*. T. Herbert Warren and Frederick Page, eds. London: Oxford University Press.

Tennyson, Lord Hallam. 1897. *Alfred, Lord Tennyson, A Memoir*, 2 vols. New York.

Veitch, John. 1878. *The History and Poetry of the Scottish Border: Their Main Features and Relations*. Glasgow.

_____. 1889. *Merlin and Other Poems*. Edinburgh.

Wordsworth, William. 1946. *The Poetical Works of William Wordsworth*. E. de Selincourt and Helen Darbishire, eds. Oxford: Claredon.

Zimmer, Heinrich. 1957. *The King and the Corpse: Tales of the Soul's Conquest of Evil*. Joseph Campbell, ed. New York: Pantheon.

Chapter Three

The Archetypal Self in Swinburne's
Tristram of Lyonesse

But peace they have that none may gain who live,
And rest about them that no love can give,
And over them, while death and life shall be,
The light and sound and darkness of the sea.
                    Swinburne, *Tristram of Lyonesse*

During Swinburne's own lifetime, George Edward Woodberry rightly
described *Tristram of Lyonesse* (1882) as "the poem most representative of
his [Swinburne's] qualities, each at its best" (1905, p. 29). But, as Ifor
Evans has noted, *Tristram* "has suffered from the first from superficial
criticism" (1966, p. 84). Evans made his comment in 1966, and since then
Swinburne's longest poem has increasingly attracted the attention of
scholars and critics, but it has not been given the recognition it deserves as
Swinburne's finest poem.[1] If we examine *Tristram of Lyonesse* from the
viewpoint of C. G. Jung's analytical psychology, we see that it is the most
psychologically satisfying of all Swinburne's poems. The achievement of
psychological wholeness (what Jung calls the Self) in the poem makes its
structure aesthetically pleasing. Tristram achieves wholeness in four
ascending stages while Iseult achieves wholeness in three ascending stages.
Together they achieve the archetypal Self.

I

According to Jung, visionary literature reveals the archetypal symbols of
the collective unconscious. Moved by an autonomous complex, the artist
brings to consciousness these symbols so that contemporary humanity may
be psychically educated or balanced. In other words, visionary work compensates for contemporary imbalance, bringing up images which society
lacks but needs, "that unconscious element of which the contemporary mental atmosphere had most need" (Jung, quoted by Philipson 1973, p. 130).

That Swinburne's *Poems and Ballads, First Series* shocked Victorian society in the mid-1860s is well known. Such was the public outcry that demands were made for the prosecution for "obscenity" of both the poet and his publisher (Henderson 1974, p. 118). Swinburne became a hero to the young, who "saw in him a literary and political revolutionary, whose anathemas were directed both against the effete autocracy of Napoleon III and against the homespun moralizing of [Tennyson's] *In Memoriam*" (Thomas 1979, p. 110). Clearly, *Poems and Ballads* compensated for not only Victorian prudery but also Victorian political and poetical conservatism.

As I indicated in my last chapter, *Tristram of Lyonesse* also compensated for contemporary imbalance and is thus, like *Poems and Ballads*, visionary art in the Jungian sense. Theodore Watts-Dunton, to whom *Tristram* is dedicated, worried that the public might react against "a poem so amatory in tone" (quoted by Thomas 1979, p. 212). And indeed he had grounds for his fears of prosecution, incredible as it may seem to readers of the latter twentieth century. One of Swinburne's publishers, Henry Vizetelly, had actually been sent to prison for three months at the age of seventy for publishing French authors such as Maupassant and Zola, whose work contained "amatory" sections not unlike those to be found in *Tristram of Lyonesse* (ibid., p. 209–213). Unfortunately, Swinburne chose to solve the potential problem "by padding out one hundred and seventy pages of *Tristram* with two hundred pages of other poems which were unobjectionable, except in aesthetic terms" (ibid., p. 213). These inferior poems, often embarrassingly sentimental verses about children, are in what Jung calls the "psychological" mode. Although they are of little interest to the literary critic, they did help prevent the feared prosecution.

Tristram compensates not only for Victorian prudery, but also for the lack of a firm religious faith. *Tristram* demonstrates the successful completion of the individuation process, a process that provides the same psychic satisfaction genuine religious or spiritual experience offers. Indeed, because Swinburne's *Tristram of Lyonesse* is the finest and most complete example in his verse of the successful completion of individuation, it is his best and most "religious" poem. It is compensatory or visionary in that it offered the Victorians (and in fact offers us) an alternative to traditional religion, faith in which many Victorians had lost but for which they had found no adequate substitute.[2]

The process of individuation is similar to the traditional hero's cycle, which begins with a "call" (von Franz 1964, pp. 166–167).[3] The first major archetypal figure from the collective unconscious to be realized is the shadow. The shadow is that part of the psyche which is not developed and which is usually not even recognized. It can be negative or positive, but is more often negative or "evil." The next archetypal symbol to be encountered is, for a man, the anima, for a woman, the animus. These are images of the contrasexual in each individual. They are images of the soul and of the unconscious itself, and they, like all the archetypes, can be positive or negative. The culmination of the process is realization of the Self — complete psychic balance, sometimes seen as a "centering."[4] Each stage of individuation is achieved through much pain and struggle and each new plateau is reached, as with the traditional hero, only after a symbolic death and rebirth. Further, individuation is a continuing process, or struggle, and is never completed until death, if then.

II

The ultimate achievement of Selfhood, or individuation, for Tristram and Iseult is foreshadowed in the prelude of *Tristram of Lyonesse*. Love, the overriding theme of the prelude, is the force that will draw the opposites of anima and animus together. It is analogous to what Jung calls psychic energy or libido; it is conceived as the energy that flows between all opposites, including sexual opposites, and which unites them:

> Love, that is first and last of all things made,
> The light that has the living world for shade,
> The spirit that for temporal veil has on
> The souls of all men woven in unison,
> One fiery raiment with all lives inwrought
> And lights of sunny and starry deed and thought,
> And alway through new act and passion new
> Shines the divine same body and beauty through,
> The body spiritual of fire and light
> That is to worldly noon as noon to night . . .
>
> (Swinburne 1904, vol. 4, p. 7)

Love combines the opposites of first/last, light/shade, noon/night so that "souls of all men [are] woven in unison." The "divine same body . . . The body spiritual" echoes Blake's "naked human form divine," which Swinburne comments upon in *William Blake: A Critical Essay* (1867): "the divine nature is not greater than the human; (they are one from eternity, sundered by the separative creation or fall, severed into type and antitype by bodily generation, but to be made one again when life and death shall both have died)" (Swinburne 1970, pp. 154–155). It is love which will lead "these twain to the lifeless light of night" (Swinburne 1904, p. 8) to once

again unite the divine with the human. John D. Rosenberg has noted that
Swinburne is "obsessed by the moment when one thing shades off into its
opposite, or when contraries fuse" (1968, p. xxxi). And it is precisely the
joining of opposites that the process of individuation is concerned with.
The central tension in *Tristram* is between opposites, opposites that either
have to be conquered (as in the shadow figures Tristram must fight —
Iseult's uncle, Palamede, Urgan, and the eight knights of Canto VIII) or
brought together. In the prelude, love unites the false opposites of flesh
and spirit:

> Love, that is flesh upon the spirit of man
> And spirit within the flesh whence breath began . . .

> (Swinburne 1904, p. 7)

Swinburne here is playing with the idea behind the Latin word *anima*,
which means the soul of man as well as the breath of life and the air or
wind; the opposite is, of course, the corpus, the body or flesh. Jung's use of
the word *anima* stems from its Latin (and Greek, *anemos* or "wind")
meaning (Jung 1933, p. 181). In regard to the passage I have just quoted,
Swinburne's comment on Blake again applies equally to his own poem.
Blake's faith, Swinburne tells us, was "grounded . . . on an equal reverence
for spirit and flesh as the two sides or halves of a completed creature"
(Swinburne 1970, p. 96).[5] The same idea is voiced by Jung, who says that
"the distinction between mind and body is an artificial dichotomy" (1933,
p. 74). If "modern man" is "in search of a soul," it is because his nature is
neurotically split, and to compensate for this dissociation visionary literature is produced.[6] Swinburne's *Tristram*, then, was an unconscious
attempt to compensate for the late Victorian preoccupation with the
material — the physical — at the expense of the spiritual.

For Tristram and Iseult, the ultimate uniting of the human and the
divine, the flesh and the spirit, and the conscious with the unconscious (the
ego with the anima/animus) can only come through death. And love is the
agent that brings this about. Love

> Led these twain to the life of tears and fire;
> Through many and lovely days and much delight
> Led these twain to the lifeless life of night.

> (Swinburne 1904, p. 8)

Through a process of "tears and fire," through, that is, great struggle, the two lovers are led paradoxically to a "lifeless life." They achieve their own unique Selfhood:

> Hath not love
> Made for all these their sweet particular air
> To shine in, their own beams and names to bear,
> Their ways to wander and their wards to keep,
> Till story and song and glory and all things sleep?
> Hath he not plucked from death of lovers dead
> Their musical soft memories, and kept red
> The rose of their remembrance in men's eyes . . .
>
> (Ibid., p. 9)

Swinburne is saying that Tristram and Iseult maintain their uniqueness in the annals of literature: from "the age of Dante" to Ercildoune (Swinburne 1904, vol. I, p. xviii) to Swinburne's own poem: "yet I too, / I have the heart to follow, many or few / Be the feet gone before me" (ibid., p. 15). In sum, Tristram and Iseult are examples par excellence of the achievement of the archetypal Self.

The theme of love runs throughout the poem, but it is especially emphasized again in the invocations to Love (with a capital "L") which begin Canto VI ("Joyous Gard") and Canto VIII ("The Last Pilgrimage"). In the invocation to "Joyous Gard," Love again corresponds to the libido, which draws the opposites of anima/animus together:

> A little time, O Love, a little light,
> A little hour for ease before the night.
> Sweet Love, that art so bitter; foolish Love,
> Whom wise men know for wiser, and thy dove
> More subtle than the serpent; for thy sake
> These pray thee for a little beam to break,
> A little grace to help them, lest men think
> Thy servants have but hours like tears to drink.
>
> (Ibid., p. 95)

But Love here is more than libido (or psychic energy); it is itself an archetype of overwhelming power. We might say that Swinburne is giving us, in his story of Tristram and Iseult, the archetype of Ideal Love: the pair are Love's "servants," and Love is conceived as divine — as if the Greek *Eros*.[7]

Further, Love has the paradoxical nature which always characterizes the archetype: it is both sweet and bitter, both foolish and wise. As a unity (in the lovers combined), it conjoins in the spiritual symbol of the dove the subtlety of the chthonic serpent.

The lovers are united, for the second time, at Joyous Gard, but at the beginning of "The Last Pilgrimage" they are separated again. Their period of "ease" and "rest" is over. Once more there is disunity between the opposites. Love's "dove," symbolic of the spirit, is "spell-stricken by the serpent," symbolic of the chthonic, the material. But the final union of the two lovers is foreshadowed in the oxymoron "night's dawn," which appears in the invocation to Love of Canto VIII (ibid., p. 122).

As I have indicated, this final union is possible only in death. It is well known that Swinburne often viewed death positively, as, for example, in "The Garden of Proserpine" and "The Triumph of Time." But death in these poems does not bring unity; it is, as it were, an escape from living. In *Tristram*, however, death brings psychic unity. In another invocation to Love in "Joyous Gard," we learn that Tristram and Iseult have been Love's servants "many a year" (ibid., p. 100), but they will not die in old age: "Death shall not take them drained of dear true life / Already, sick or stagnant from the strife" (ibid., p. 101). On the subject of death, Jung writes "that the highest summit of life can be expressed through the symbolism of death, for any growing beyond one-self means death, is a well known fact" (quoted by Aronson 1972, p. 33). A comment by Alex Aronson helps to clarify Jung's view of death:

> In Jungian therapeutic work the process of healing includes an acceptance of the phenomenon of dying as part of the process of living. If death is found to be the sole remedy — not as an escape from but as a fulfillment of self — then it is the physician's task to help the patient in facing his death as he has helped him in his daily confrontation with life. (Ibid., p. 34)

The most complete self-fulfillment in Tristram can come only through death — not a lonely death in old age, but an early death when both anima and animus can be united. Death, therefore, is a positive achievement: it is the highest summit of life. Just as the body will not be sick or stagnant when it dies, so the spirit will be whole.

III

The call to individuation for Tristram and Iseult is objectified in the love potion they drink in Canto I, "The Sailing of the Swallow." The drinking of the love potion takes place in the sunlight, symbolic of consciousness, after a storm, symbolic of the unconscious. Already we have a metaphoric death and rebirth for the new lovers. In analytical psychology, if a synthesis is achieved between the ego and an archetypal symbol, it is brought about by the transcendent function — a function that forces "the energy of the opposites into a common channel" (Jung 1921, p. 480). The love potion, besides being a call, symbolizes this transcendent function because it brings about a seemingly inexplicable change. After drinking it, Tristram and Iseult find that love is fated to drive them into the unity of the Self. They are no longer separate or innocent; they are forever to be engaged in a search for unity:

> Their heads neared, and their hands were drawn in one,
> And they saw dark, though still the unsunken sun
> Far through fine rain shot fire into the south;
> And their four lips became one burning mouth.
>
> (Swinburne 1904, p. 42)

As with the lovers in Dante Gabriel Rossetti's painting *Paolo and Francesca*, Tristram and Iseult are joined in the dark world of the unconscious with all its terrors for the conscious mind.[8] It is no accident that the number four — in analytical psychology a number of unity — is here viewed as one, for in the second canto, "The Queen's Pleasance," the lovers will know the first sustained fulfillment of the Self.

Even before drinking the love potion, Tristram has had his first successful encounter with the shadow archetype. Taking his inspiration from Malory's *Morte Darthur*, Swinburne has the King of Ireland demand, like Minos, a tribute from the King of Cornwall. Like Theseus, Tristram slays the Minotaur (symbolized by Iseult's uncle), thus freeing King Mark of the tribute. The uncle symbolizes the beast within which must be slain. After meeting and slaying the shadow, Tristram is ready to encounter the anima on the next stage of his individuation process. That Iseult is the anima for Tristram is suggested by her healing him with "holy remedies / Made by her mother's magic in strange hours / Out of live roots and life-compelling flowers" (Swinburne 1904, p. 21). The

FIGURE 2
Paolo and Francesca (1862), by D. G. Rossetti:
This is the painting Swinburne had in mind when he wrote *Tristram of Lyonesse.*

anima, symbolizing a man's unconscious, is here coupled with the earthly, chthonic world (also symbolic of the feminine), and their psychic power to heal is graphically shown.

But Tristram and Iseult do not achieve Selfhood until they are also united physically, after drinking the love potion. Before this first experience of the Self, Tristram has again to encounter the shadow, this time in the figure of Palamede. Palamede is, like Tristram, a minstrel, and he is, in fact, second only to Tristram on the harp (ibid., p. 48). In a scene reminiscent of Herod Antipas and Salome (which Swinburne derives in part from Sir Walter Scott's edition of *Sir Tristrem*), a drunken Mark, pleased with Palamede's entertainment on the harp, promises to give the harpist anything he might crave. He craves Iseult (Tristram is not present). Rather than break his royal promise, Mark allows Palamede to take Iseult. Thus, the scene is prepared for Tristram's first major struggle for the anima and hence the Self. Palamede is too ashamed of his disloyalty to have intercourse with Iseult, but Tristram, nevertheless, in true knightly fashion, comes to rescue his damsel in distress. A vividly drawn battle follows, and Tristram is, of course, the victor.

Leaving the conquered Palamede "where he lay," Tristram and Iseult retreat deeper into the unconscious — to a woodland bower. What ensues Swinburne calls "my modest effort to paint a sylvan scene of unpretending enjoyment by moonlight" (1959–1962, vol. 4, p. 239), "The Queen's Pleasance," in other words. For three months the lovers know "that sweet wonder of the twain made one" (Swinburne 1904, p. 37); they feel "Sense into sense and spirit in spirit melt" (ibid., p. 56). Herbert Dingle's comment, in *Science and Literary Criticism*, is apposite here: "Sex love for him [Swinburne] is a fusion — body and soul — of the lover and his mate, in which identity, individuality and outline are lost" (1949, p. 141). The syzygy of anima/animus, as Jung terms it, has resulted in the fusion to which Dingle refers. A wholeness, a *coniunctio oppositorium*, has resulted in this first extended realization of the Self for Tristram and Iseult.[9] But the resolution of the opposites has not yet caused loss of identity — it never does for the living individuated person; instead, they realize a self-fulfillment never previously known. Only in the final assimilation of opposites in death will there be the loss of individual identity.

Mark's discovery of the two, with Tristram's sword between them, cuts the two lovers off from the world of the unconscious and forces them back into the world of consciousness. In this world the lovers are split and they suffer consciously, as does the Iseult portrayed in William Morris's painting, *La Belle Iseult*(1858). We see this in the first part of Canto III, "Tristram in Brittany," in Tristram's long philosophical monologue, and

FIGURE 3
La Belle Iseult (1858), by William Morris

William Morris's only extant painting, *La Belle Iseult* (also called *Queen Guenevere*) shows Iseult longing for union with Tristram and demonstrates, once again, the powerful collective appeal of the Arthurian tales for the Victorians.

in Canto V, "Iseult at Tintagel," in Iseult's agonizing prayer.[10] In Canto III, Tristram, now a more unified individual, realizes the paradox of the archetype:

> We have loved and slain each other, and love yet.
> Slain; for we live not surely, being in twain:
> In her I lived, and in me she is slain,
> Who loved me that I brought her to her doom,
> Who loved her that her love might be my tomb.
>
> (Swinburne 1904, p. 60)

A little later, he says that "The sunlight . . . Must die that she being dead may live again" (ibid., p. 61). In other words, the two lovers have gone through a symbolic death in the unconscious and have been reborn with a new awareness, an expanded consciousness. They have gone through, as it were, an initiation rite.

Like Tristram in Canto III, Iseult consciously struggles with her psychic problem, having been split off from the contrasexual. She, too, realizes that she has gone through a symbolic death and rebirth — the religious process of transformation to which, in a different context, Emma Jung refers in an essay on the animus (1972, p. 8):

> And time is long since last I felt the touch,
> The sweet touch of my lover, hand and breath,
> In such delight as puts delight to death,
> Burns my soul through, till spirit and soul and sense,
> In the sharp grasp of the hour, with violence
> Died, and again through pangs of violent birth
> Lived, and laughed out with refluent might of mirth;
> Laughed each on other and shuddered into one.
>
> (Swinburne 1904, pp. 88–89)

The sense of psychic fusion of the opposites here could not be stronger. Just before this passage, in a phrase which echoes Catherine's about Heathcliff in *Wuthering Heights*, Iseult had come to the ultimate realization that, "I am he indeed . . . and he is I" (ibid., p. 88). She consciously understands her relationship to the unconscious symbol of the animus. Emma Jung writes that "with the animus, the emphasis . . . is on knowledge, and especially understanding. It is the function of the animus to give the meaning rather than the image [of the unconscious]" (1972, p.

26). Clearly, the animus has given Iseult much more than an inkling of her relation to the unconscious.

Between the cantos I have been discussing is Canto IV, in which Tristram becomes entrapped in "The Maiden Marriage" with Iseult of Brittany. She is unwittingly the archetypal temptress for Tristram at the end of Canto III, but her success in this role is not at all gratifying for her. Her union with Tristram is a false union, and the physical act of love — in *Tristram*, a symbol of the Self — is absent. The canto opens with an ominous anticipation of the wedding:

> Spring watched her last moon burn and fade with May
> While the days deepened toward a bridal day.
> And on her snowbright hand the ring was set
> While in the maiden's ear the song's word yet
> Hovered, that hailed as love's own queen by name
> Iseult: and in her heart the word was flame;
> A pulse of light, a breath of tender fire,
> Too dear for doubt, too driftless for desire.

> (Swinburne 1904, p. 75)

The song, of course, is Tristram's, sung for Iseult of Ireland. Iseult of Brittany has not unsurprisingly misinterpreted it as referring to herself. She is in the spring of her life: innocent and naive like the Irish Iseult of Canto I; yet her psychic struggle ends, not in wholeness, but in disillusion, bitterness, and hate. Her engagement ring should have been a mandala, a symbol of completeness, but Tristram is not a part of that completeness. He is part of another ring of which this Iseult is unaware:

> She saw not how by hap at home-coming
> Fell from her new lord's hand a royal ring,
> Whereon he looked, and felt the pulse astart
> Speak passion in her faith-forsaken heart.

> (Ibid.)

Symbolically, Tristram is half of this royal ring of which Iseult of Ireland is the other half. In his desire to fill the vacancy caused by their separation, Tristram is willing to link with a counterfeit Iseult.

After she realizes what her fate is, the Breton Iseult becomes neurotic. She suffers from what Jung calls "a dissociation of personality" (1968, p. 188).[11] She is split off from the masculine part of herself, but at the same time becomes paradoxically possessed by those "masculine" traits characteristic of the negative side of the animus. She is, in short, animus-possessed.[12] Thus, in Canto VII, "The Wife's Vigil," she is "parched with blasts of thought" and "withered with wind of evil will" (Swinburne 1904, p. 113). The psychic energy that has been directed outward in Iseult's psyche has also activated the symbol of the animus in its negative manifestation. Emma Jung explains this phenomenon thus: "Possessed of the energy that has flowed back into the unconscious, the animus figure becomes autonomous, so powerful, indeed, that it can overwhelm the conscious ego, and thus finally dominate the whole personality" (1972, p. 6). This is exactly what has happened to Iseult of Brittany. She invokes only the terrible aspect of God, the Father:

> How long, till thou do justice, and my wrong
> Stand expiate? O long-suffering judge, how long?
> Shalt thou not put him in mine hand one day
> Whom I so loved, to spare not but to slay?

> (Swinburne 1904, p. 117)

Iseult herself wants to be the instrument of God's judgment. In wanting to slay Tristram (and in ultimately accomplishing that goal indirectly), the Breton Iseult is the shadow of the Irish Iseult (that part which would destroy him) as well as the negative anima for Tristram.

IV

One of the reasons for the Breton Iseult's bitterness and hate is that Tristram has been gone from her. He has, indeed, met with the Irish Iseult at Launcelot's castle, Joyous Gard, and has for the second time achieved Selfhood.[13] Swinburne describes their experience thus:

> Within the full deep glorious tower that stands
> Between the wild sea and the broad wild lands
> Love led and gave them quiet: and they drew
> Life like a God's life in each wind that blew,
> And took their rest, and triumphed. Day by day
> The mighty moorlands and the sea-walls grey,
> The brown bright waters of green fells that sing
> One song to rocks and flowers and birds on wing,
> Beheld the joy and glory that they had,
> Passing, and how the whole world made them glad,

> And their great love was mixed with all things great,
> As life being lovely, and yet being strong like fate.

(1904, p. 102)

The tower (or the castle) is a symbol of the Self seen in its aspect of being the center; it is "Between the wild sea and the broad wild lands."[14] Again the human and the divine are united, for the lovers "drew / Life like a God's life." Music ("One song") and love draw the opposites together, and Tristram and Iseult are truly one with themselves and with nature: "their great love was mixed with all things great."

Here at Joyous Gard, Tristram and Iseult discuss the fate of another Arthurian pair: Merlin and Nimue, the only other pair in Swinburne's Arthurian canon who fully achieve the end of the individuation process. Nimue (Tennyson's "Vivien" and Arnold's "Vivian" in their respective Tristram poems) has "sealed . . . [Merlin] fast with sleep" in Brittany. Of the important writers from the Middle Ages to his own era, Swinburne is the only one to view Merlin's fate as unqualifiedly positive. This is because he wants Merlin and Nimue to parallel Tristram and Iseult: both pairs achieve a state of psychic health — Selfhood, in other words, as I demonstrated in Chapter Two. Merlin, says Tristram, "Takes his strange rest at heart of Broceliande" (Swinburne 1904, p. 106). He has been reborn through death to become one with nature: "in the spirit of earth /
His spirit of life [is] reborn to mightier birth / And mixed with things of elder life than ours" (ibid., p. 107). The Selfhood of Merlin and Nimue resembles the future fate of Tristram and Iseult:

> Yea, heart in heart is molten, hers and his,
> Into the world's heart and the soul that is
> Beyond or sense or vision; and their breath
> Stirs the soft springs of deathless life and death,
> Death that bears life, and change that brings forth seed
> Of life to death and death to life indeed,
> As blood recircling through the unsounded veins
> Of earth and heaven with all their joys and pains.
> Ah, that when love shall laugh no more nor weep
> We too, we too might hear that song and sleep!

(Ibid., pp. 107–108)

The lovers are "Beyond or sense or vision" because the opposites of matter and spirit have returned to their primordial unity. In the same way, the opposites of "earth and heaven" and "joys and pains" are joined. The "blood recircling" suggests a mandalic unity, but it also suggests psychic energy (libido) which has drawn the opposites together: blood here is a symbol of that energy.[15]

Iseult concurs with Tristram's sentiment, expressed in the last couplet of the above passage:

> "Yes," said Iseult, "some joy it were to be
> Lost in the sun's light and the all-girdling sea,
> Mixed with the winds and woodlands, and to bear
> Part in the large life of the quickening air,
> And the sweet earth's, our mother. . . ."

(Ibid., p. 108)

Fisher rightly identifies the sun as "one of the pervasive unifiers" in the poem, but in the end the sun must, as in this passage, be coupled with the sea for full unity to be attained (1972, p. 515). Iseult wonders if she, like Nimue, has the healing power of the anima (the power "To heal men's hearts as earth is healed by spring"). She asks Tristram, "what gift can I give thee?" and decides that at least she has not given him "shame" (Swinburne 1904, p. 109). Tristram answers: "O very woman, god at once and child, / What ails thee to desire of me once more / The assurance that thou hadst in heart before?" (ibid., p. 109–110). Iseult has given him "life, not death." She has given him, that is, an expanded consciousness.

At Joyous Gard, Tristram and Iseult are together in wholeness for the last time in life. Iseult must return to Tintagel and her husband, King Mark, because Arthur has called upon Tristram to fight the giant, Urgan, "For succour toward his vassal Triamour, / King in wild Wales, now spoiled of all his power" (ibid., p. 124). Both Tristram and Iseult have, in other words, to return to their conscious roles in life, what Jung calls the personae (1953, pp. 167–168): Iseult as Queen of Cornwall, Tristram as a knight of the Round Table. In going as a "pilgrim" to do battle with Urgan, Tristram is not only acting out his role as knight; he is also again meeting the personification of the archetypal shadow. It is as if he were reliving his youth:

> Tristram by dense hills and deepening vales
> Rode through the wild glad wastes of glorious Wales,
> High-hearted with desire of happy fight

59

And strong in soul with merrier sense of might
Than since the fair first years that hailed him knight. . . .

(Swinburne 1904, p. 125)

Tristram wants "To pluck once more as out of circling fire / Fame, the broad flower whose breath makes death more sweet / Than roses crushed by love's receding feet" (ibid., p. 125). With the self-awareness and extended consciousness he has gained from his experience in love, Tristram is better prepared now than he was as a youth to fight the shadow. Urgan, as is often the case with the shadow, is bestial: he has "A beast's broad laugh of wolfish will" (ibid., p. 127). After a lengthy battle, Tristram prevails. Through a public act, he has conquered again his own shadow and can thus again achieve a state of psychic wholeness, this time without Iseult.

This third, penultimate achievement of Selfhood for Tristram takes place in Canto VIII, "The Last Pilgrimage," in the sea off Brittany; and this time the anima is symbolized by the sea, which is compared to a "bride" joining with "the young sun" (ibid., p. 137). Shortly before, Tristram himself has been compared to the sun (ibid., p. 134). Once more Tristram is in the unconscious; he has been sleeping on the beach, and he wakes "ere the sun spake summons." He is about to plunge naked into the sea in a passage that is, as George Woodberry says, "unique in literature" (1905, p. 99).[16] Swinburne compares Tristram to a boy before he takes his dip:

as a boy
That leaps up light to wrestle with the sea
For pure heart's gladness and large ecstasy,
Up sprang the might of Tristram; and his soul
Yearned for delight within him, and waxed whole
As a young child's with rapture of the hour
That brought his spirit and all the world to flower,
And all the bright blood in his veins beat time
To the wind's clarion and the water's chime
That called him and he followed it and stood
On the sand's verge before the grey great flood
Where the white hurtling heads of waves that met
Rose unsaluted of the sunrise yet.

(Swinburne 1904, pp. 136–137)

In a state of unity now, Tristram is "full-souled" and "whole." He is like a newborn child who has just come from what Erich Neumann calls the uroboric state of wholeness in the womb. It is the "dawn state" (just as the day in this passage is about to dawn) in which consciousness is about to emerge (Neumann 1954, pp. 11–12). Reaching out for further self-awareness, Tristram answers a call from "the wind's clarion and the water's chime."

In having this protagonist jump naked into the sea, Swinburne probably has in mind Blake's "naked human form divine" (Swinburne 1970, p. 154) who is a symbol of the unity of man and God ("God is man, and man God" (ibid., p. 155)) — a symbol, that is, of the Self. Like the castle, Joyous Gard, Tristram stands in the center "between the sea's edge and the sea." He is "naked and godlike . . . [the] Child of heroic earth and heavenly sea, / The flower of all men." Then he jumps:

> with a cry of love that rang
> As from a trumpet golden-mouthed, he sprang,
> As toward a mother's where his head might rest
> Her child rejoicing, toward the strong sea's breast
> That none may gird nor measure . . .
>
> (Swinburne 1904, p. 138)

The sea is personified as a woman, and Tristram makes love to it, taking

> the bright breast of the wave to his
> And on his lips the sharp sweet minute's kiss
> Given of the wave's lip for a breath's space curled
> And pure as at the daydawn of the world.
>
> (Ibid., pp. 138–139)

The union of anima/animus has transcended the actual physical act of sex and become a mystical experience. Tristram is in harmony now with "the tune of life," the "music" that brings wholeness. He is reborn into "a new-begotten son / Between the live sea and the living sun" (ibid., p. 139). Selfhood is again pictured as a process of centering.

This passage has puzzled critics who have missed its meaning. Howard Maynadier, for example, calls it "an especially long digression" (1907, p. 374). But if we consider that four is, for Jung, the archetypal number of wholeness, then the sea-dip episode is entirely appropriate and even necessary to the structure of the poem. It is the third of four ascending stages of Selfhood for Tristram. In it, he experiences a mystical unity with nature and the divine. Iseult, on the other hand, reaches Selfhood in three ascending stages, for three is more often the number of unity for the feminine. The tripartite Kore figure, for example, is a symbol of the feminine Self (Jung and Kerényi 1963, p. 156).

V

When Tristram returns to Brittany from Joyous Gard, he encounters a very interesting character, one who does not figure at all in Arnold's *Tristram and Iseult* (1852) or in Tennyson's "The Last Tournament" (1872), and who, in modern versions, is usually not associated with the Tristram legend.[17] This is a younger Tristram who appeals to the older Tristram to help him recover his lady, who has been kidnapped by a knight and his "Seven brethren" (Swinburne 1904, p. 133). The obvious psychological interpretation of this younger Tristram is that he is an image of Tristram's former self (with a small "s" to distinguish him from the archetypal Self). He is a form of the shadow figure since he mirrors the Tristram who was. Like the early Tristram, this one is innocent and naive. He laments, for example, that the Breton Iseult "Lacks her lord and light of wedded life" (ibid., p. 134). Also like the early Tristram (as well as the present Tristram of Lyonesse), this younger Tristram is separated from the contrasexual. In agreeing to assist this Tristram, the older knight is doing his chivalric duty. But he is also attempting to unite the opposites of anima and animus outwardly or in the conscious — a way that, for him, is no longer possible. As if the unconscious were sending him this message, Tristram fails. He succeeds in slaying the eight knights, but the younger Tristram is himself slain (ibid., p. 142); this is after Tristram's naked sea-dip. The message is that Tristram must forever sever the past with its outward solutions. He must look for wholeness now only from the spiritual, not from any sexual attachment.

Having died to his former self, having slain the shadow for the last time, and having been wounded in the very place on his body where he had first been wounded, Tristram is again in need of healing. This time the only health he will find will be psychic health as he and Iseult return to an undifferentiated state of unity in the final canto, "The Sailing of the Swan."

Canto IX opens with a long — perhaps too long — passage on Fate which is not unlike the passage on Love that opens the prelude. Like Love, Fate is the primordial force that fuses all into unity:

Fate, that was born ere spirit and flesh were made,
The fire that fills man's life with light and shade;
The power beyond all godhead which puts on
All forms of multitudinous unison,
A raiment of eternal change inwrought
With shapes and hues more subtly spun than thought,
Where all things old bear fruit of all things new
And one deep chord throbs all the music through,
Inseparable as reverberate day from night . . .

(Ibid., p. 144)

Like Love, Fate here is analogous to libido, the psychic energy which constantly flows between opposites — hence, the "eternal change." Music again is intimately associated with the harmonious union of such opposites as shadow / light and day / night.

Through Fate, "life" will find "no discord in the tune with death" (ibid.). And "birth and death [will] be one in sight of light" (ibid., p. 145). Birth and death are archetypally alike because they both represent threshold states of being where the consciousness has, with birth, just emerged or, with death, is about to be submerged back into the uroboric state of unconsciousness where all needs are met and all is at one. Like Fate, Truth will trample "the head of Fear" (ibid., p. 147), so that the end of the individual fates of Tristram and Iseult is once more presented as a positive factor and one not to be feared.

Tristram has now waited "Three dim days through, three slumberless nights long" since he was wounded. His "strong man's soul now sealed indeed with pain" is a "Prisoner within the fleshly dungeon-dress / Sore chafed and wasted with its weariness" (ibid., p. 148). If, as I contend, *Tristram of Lyonesse* is visionary literature which offers a compensatory alternative to traditional religion for the late Victorians, then Tristram may be said to be the Christ figure in the poem.[18] His individuation process symbolizes a kind of salvation or redemption that many Victorians could not find in Christianity as they understood it. Christ's body lies in the grave three days while his spirit harrows hell. After three days his body is resurrected. Tristram, on the other hand, lies three days consciously waiting for death; his hell is on earth, and only death releases him.

In a well-known episode of the legend, Tristram tells Ganhardine, his brother-in-law, to sail in the *Swan* to Cornwall to bring Iseult back to him. He is to fly a white sail if Iseult is returning with him and a black one if she is not. The two sails are another indication that in *Tristram* we are dealing with the problem of contraries, of opposites. Clearly, they are symbolic of the two Iseults: the positive anima (the white sail) and the negative anima (the black sail). The black sail is symbolic of the Breton Iseult because she lies in telling Tristram that the ship is flying it (Swinburne 1904, p. 160). She has a "virgin lust for vengeance" because she has never consciously accommodated the unconscious figure of the animus. As Emma Jung says, "There are unconscious contents that struggle to become conscious and . . . revenge themselves if this is not taken into account" (1972, p. 79). The animus in Iseult of Brittany avenges himself by possessing her as the negative side of the archetype, and she thus seals the fate of Tristram and, consequently, the fate of Iseult of Ireland (or Cornwall). Ironically, the "black" appears to triumph when in fact the "white" triumphs.

Tristram and Iseult at last find peace in the experience of the Self: "The stroke of love's own hand felt last and best / Gave them deliverance to perpetual rest." Just as Tristram dies, his lover arrives and dies herself as she kisses him: "And their four lips became one silent mouth." As in "The Sailing of the Swallow," the number four is associated with the unity of the lovers. They are now "From the bondage and the fear of time set free" (ibid., p. 160). They are at one with themselves and with nature:

> but their sleep
> Hath round it like a raiment all the deep;
> No change or gleam or gloom of sun or rain,
> But all time long the might of all the main
> Spread around them as round earth soft heaven is spread
> And peace more strong than death round all the dead

> (Ibid., p. 161)

Although Mark (who has been enlightened about the love potion by a posthumously discovered note in "Tristram's hand") buries the two in a chapel in Tintagel, their final resting place is the sea, which had "swallowed [the] wall and tower" of the chapel (ibid., pp. 162–163).

W. H. Auden has remarked that, for the romantic, "The only possible place of peace . . . lies under the waters" (1950, p. 24). From the Jungian point of view, this means that the sea is the primal place of unity—of "undifferentiated nature," to use the phrase of another archetypal critic.[19] But before this final harmonious peace, Tristram and Iseult in the chapel are "wedded under moon and sun" in a *hieros gamos*, a "sacred wedding" (the chapel connotes the sacredness) which is another symbol of the Self. Selfhood is even more complete under the sea: "Nor where they sleep shall moon or sunlight shine." The sea, then, is the great primordial uniter of all opposites, and Swinburne ends his finest poem, as he ends so many of his other poems, with the word "sea":

> But peace they have that none may gain who live,
> And rest about them that no love can give,
> And over them, while death and life shall be,
> The light and sound and darkness of the sea.

(Swinburne 1904, p. 163)

Tristram and Iseult have completed their archetypal struggle for the Self and have been immortalized by the finest Victorian poem devoted to them. As visionary literature, *Tristram of Lyonesse* brings to our modern consciousness, as it brought to the Victorian collective consciousness, an example of how each modern person may be successful in his or her individual struggle for the Self.

Notes

1. See, for example, John R. Reed (1966), Kerry McSweeney (1968), Benjamin Franklin Fisher IV (1972), and Nicolas Tredell (1982). I agree with Tredell, who says of *Tristram*: "in its scale and archetypal resonance it can only be compared to D. H. Lawrence" (p. 97). Tredell also declares that as a singer, "Tristram is Orpheus, archetype of the poet, and the model for Swinburne himself" (p. 98). As a harpist and singer and in his archetypal hero's journey to the Self, Tristram is indeed like Orpheus. However, Tredell uses the term archetype loosely, without clearly defining it. See also David G. Riede, *Swinburne: A Study of Romantic Mythmaking* (Charlottesville, Va.: University Press of Virginia, 1978), cited in Chapter Two, note 2.

2. Benjamin Fisher points out that *Tristram* "is . . . a visionary poem, for Swinburne tells us in the 'Prelude' that this is *his* vision of the immortal pair of lovers" (1972, p. 511). Obviously Fisher uses the term visionary in a different context from Jung, but the more traditional meaning that Fisher employs is the basis upon which Jung invented his own unique meaning.

3. I am referring here to the second half of the individuation process, which occurs later in life. In the first half of the process, the individual must adapt to his or her outer environment. Tristram and Iseult have little problem doing so; their real problem is internal.

4. For a fuller explanation of the individuation process, see Chapter One.

5. Swinburne himself claimed to be "of the Church of Blake and Shelley" (Swinburne 1959–1962, vol. 3, p. 14).

6. Jung makes a distinction between "psyche" and "soul": "By psyche I understand the totality of all psychic processes, conscious as well as unconscious. By soul, on the other hand, I understand a clearly demarcated functional complex that can best be described as a 'personality'" (1921, p. 463). Soul can designate either persona, anima or animus, or personality. In connection with Swinburne's Tristram and Iseult, "soul" stands for the contrasexual, the "soul-image" of each as represented by the other.

7. In a recent Jungian interpretation of the Tristan and Iseult legend, based on medieval sources and published six years after an earlier version of this chapter appeared in the *Psychocultural Review* (Snider 1977), Robert A. Johnson (1983) also identifies love as an archetype. Johnson calls the archetype "love" or "romantic love," while I call it "Ideal Love." The kind of love I refer to is exceedingly rare between two human beings. It is the kind of romantic love in which the two lovers seem to have found their other halves, as in Plato's *Symposium*, where the primal beings were split into male–male, female–female, and male–female and then go seeking their other halves. In our conscious lives, rarely do two such people find each other (Johnson 1983, pp. 189-201). Unlike my interpretation, Johnson's is not intended to be a literary study. He is a Jungian analyst using what he calls the "myth" of Tristan and Iseult as a basis for "psychological insight" (ibid., p. vii).

8. Francesca appears in Swinburne's remarkable zodiac of female lovers in "Prelude," and her story closely parallels Iseult's. We know, from a letter to D. G. Rossetti (dated December 22, 1869), that Swinburne was thinking not only of the version of the Paolo and Francesca story given in Dante, but also of Rossetti's (Swinburne 1959–1962, vol. 2, p. 75).

9. See Jung 1951, p. 31. Another way of describing what has happened is to say that for Tristram, the anima (symbolized by Iseult) has been incorporated into — or joined to — his consciousness; and vice versa, for Iseult, the animus (symbolized by Tristram) has been incorporated into her consciousness. In both cases, each achieves psychic wholeness.

10. In these passages, Tristram and Iseult exercise that function of consciousness most often associated with masculinity — thinking — "the function which seeks," as Jacobi writes, "to apprehend the world and adjust to it by way of thought or cognition" (1968, p. 12). Because Tristram and Iseult are symbolic of the archetypes of the second half of the individuation process, I don't wish to place too much emphasis on their development of the functions of consciousness (thinking, feeling, sensation, intuition). These functions are important to the individual's adjustment to his or her outer environment. Their development is, however, a necessary condition to an individual's unconscious maturity. In Cantos III and V, we see a Tristram and an Iseult who have become more psychologically mature than they were at the beginning of the poem. Previously they had perceived the world mainly through the sensation function (through physical love especially). Now they perceive not only through the thinking function, but also through the feeling function, which, as Jung says, "imparts to the content a definite *value* in the sense of acceptance or rejection" (1921, p. 434).

    In Canto VI, "Joyous Gard," the lovers exercise the intuition function insofar as they intuit their death in "the all-girdling sea" (Swinburne 1904, p. 108). That Tristram and Iseult are able to exercise, to some extent, all of the functions of consciousness indicates that they are integrated personalities on the conscious level of the psyche. Their real struggle is, as I have indicated, on an unconscious level.

11. In *Two Essays on Analytical Psychology*, Jung further defines neurosis as "self-division" (1953, p. 30).

12. See *The Archetypes and the Collective Unconscious*, where Jung writes that "this transformation of personality [caused by anima- and animus-possession] gives prominence to those traits which are characteristic of the opposite sex; in man the feminine traits, and in woman the masculine" (1950a, p. 124).

13. This time Tristram has not encountered another shadow figure, but he has forsaken his false union with Iseult of Brittany. His role as her husband might be considered a shadow role for him because for him it is not natural.

14. In *The Archetypes and the Collective Unconscious*, Jung writes: "The centre [of personality] is not felt or thought of as the ego, but, if one may so express

it, as the self" (1950b, p. 357). Edward Edinger notes that the Self "often appears as a process of centering or as a process involving the union of opposites" (1968, p. 7).

15. For the blood of sacrifice as psychic energy, see Emma Jung (1972, pp. 33–34). On the conscious level, Swinburne here is giving "expression," as Margaret Reid points out, "to his own pantheistic philosophy" (1938, p. 80). But on the unconscious level he is describing the psychic fulfillment Jung calls the Self. Note, also, that in the passage just cited, music ("that song") is again a force that creates unity.

16. There are, however, parallels to, or at least anticipations of, the passage in Swinburne's own work. Compare this line from the "Hymn of Man" in *Songs Before Sunrise* (1871): "In the sea whereof centuries are waves the live God plunges and swims" (Swinburne 1904, vol. 2, p. 99); or the end of the "Epilogue" to the same volume where the swimmer in the sea is a metaphor for the man who is "Free, boundless, fearless, perfect, one" (ibid., p. 248). As Woodberry notes, "The sea . . . is his [Swinburne's] nature-symbol of liberty, of that in the spirit of all mankind which is the greatest object of human effort, the condition and the consummation of greatness in nations or men, the state of being in which they truly are at all" (1905, pp. 90–91).

17. He does not, for example, appear in Wagner's *Tristan und Isolde*, just as Iseult of Brittany does not appear in that opera.

18. In his interpretation of the Tristan legend, Johnson declares:

> The inner act required of a Western man is to affirm his own religious nature. It means to affirm seriously that the images and feelings that flow out of him in dream, fantasy, and imagination are the stuff of the divine realm, a separate order of reality distinct from his physical and personal life but equally real and equally important. He must be willing to take those images seriously, to spend time living with them, to see them as powers of great importance within himself, inhabitants of a spiritual realm that his soul transmits to him in symbol. (1983, pp. 165–166)

What applies to contemporary Western humanity applied equally to the late Victorians; and Johnson's comments about the meaning of the Tristan legend apply to both the late nineteenth and the late twentieth centuries: "What is required is not so much an external, collective religion, but an inner experience of the numinous, divine realm that is manifested through the psyche" (ibid., p. 186).

19. Elliott B. Gose, "Pure Exercise of Imagination: Archetypal Symbolism in *Lord Jim*" (1964, p. 147). *Lord Jim* is another instance where completed individuation can happen only in death. My claim here, in an earlier version of this chapter in the *Psychocultural Review*, has been criticized as a "distortion of Jungian theory" because "achieving of Self can hardly be a return to 'undifferentiated nature' " (van Meurs 1988, pp. 280–281). However, Jung,

late in his life, said "death . . . is a wedding, a *mysterium coniunctionis*. The soul attains, as it were, its missing half, it achieves wholeness" (1963, p. 314). Von Franz calls the *hieros gamos* "the final goal of individuation" (1987, p. 48). Furthermore, in *Symbols of Transformation*, Jung writes: "That the highest summit of life can be expressed through the symbolism of death is a well-known fact, for any growing beyond oneself means death." And he adds a comment that is particularly germane to *Tristram of Lyonesse*: "Love and death have not a little to do with one another" (1952, p. 285). In Swinburne's poem, we are of course dealing on the symbolic — the archetypal — level.

Works Cited

Aronson, Alex. 1972. *Psyche and Symbol in Shakespeare*. Bloomington, Ind.: Indiana University Press.

Auden, W. H. 1950. *The Enchafèd Flood: or the Romantic Iconography of the Sea*. New York: Vintage.

Dingle, Herbert. 1949. *Science and Literary Criticism*. London: Thomas Nelson.

Edinger, Edward F. 1968. An outline of analytical psychology. In *Quadrant: Notes on Analytical Psychology*, reprint I. New York: The C. G. Jung Foundation for Analytical Psychology.

Evans, Ifor. 1966. *English Poetry in the Later Nineteenth Century*. 2nd ed. London: Methuen.

Fisher, Benjamin Franklin, IV. 1972. Swinburne's *Tristram of Lyonesse* in process. *Texas Studies in Literature and Language* 14:508–528.

Gose, Elliott B., Jr. 1964. Pure Exercise of Imagination: Archetypal Symbolism in *Lord Jim*. *Publications of the Modern Language Association* 79:137–147.

Henderson, Philip. 1974. *Swinburne: Portrait of a Poet*. New York: Macmillan.

Jacobi, Jolande. 1968. *The Psychology of C. G. Jung: An Introduction with Illustrations*. Ralph Manheim, trans. New Haven: Yale University Press.

Johnson, Robert A. 1983. *WE: Understanding the Psychology of Romantic Love*. San Francisco: Harper.

Jung, C. G. 1921. *Psychological Types*. *CW*, vol. 6. Princeton, N.J.: Princeton University Press, 1971.

_____. 1933. Modern Man in Search of a Soul. W. S. Dell and Cary F. Baynes, trans. New York: Harcourt.

_____. 1950a. Concerning rebirth. *CW* 9:113–149. Princeton, N.J.: Princeton University Press, 1959.

_____. 1950b. Concerning mandala symbolism. *CW* 9i:355–384. Princeton, N.J.: Princeton University Press, 1959.

_____. 1951. *Aion: Researches into the Phenomenology of the Self. CW*, vol. 9ii. Princeton, N.J.: Princeton University Press, 1951.

_____. 1952. *Symbols of Transformation. CW*, vol. 5. Princeton, N.J.: Princeton University Press, 1956.

_____. 1953. *Two Essays on Analytical Psychology.* R. F. C. Hull, trans. New York: World.

_____. 1963. Memories, Dreams, Reflections. Richard and Clara Winston, trans. Aniela Jaffé, ed. New York: Vintage.

_____. 1968. *Analytical Psychology, Its Theory and Practice: The Tavistock Lectures.* New York: Vintage.

Jung, C. G., and Kerényi, C. 1963. *Essays on a Science of Mythology: The Myth of the Divine Child and the Mysteries of Eleusis.* R. F. C. Hull, trans. Princeton, N.J.: Princeton University Press.

Jung, Emma. 1972. *Animus and Anima.* Cary F. Baynes and Hildegard Nagel, trans. Zürich: Spring Publications.

Maynadier, Howard. 1907. *The Arthur of the English Poets.* Boston: Houghton.

McSweeney, Kerry. 1968. The structure of Swinburne's "Tristram of Lyonesse." *Queen's Quarterly* 75:690–702.

Neumann, Erich. 1954. *The Origins and History of Consciousness.* R. F. C. Hull, trans. Princeton, N.J.: Princeton University Press.

Philipson, Morris. 1973. *Outline of a Jungian Aesthetics.* Evanston, Ill.: Northwestern University Press.

Reed, John R. 1966. Swinburne's *Tristram of Lyonesse*: the poet-lover's song of love. *Victorian Poetry* 4:99–120.

Reid, Margaret J. C. 1938. *The Arthurian Legend, Comparison of Treatment in Modern and Medieval Literature: A Study in the Literary Value of Myth and Legend.* Edinburgh: Oliver and Boyd.

Riede, David G. 1978. *Swinburne: A Study of Romantic Mythmaking.* Charlottesville, Va.: University Press of Virginia.

Rosenberg, John D., ed. 1968. *Swinburne: Selected Poetry and Prose.* New York: Modern Library.

Snider, Clifton, 1977. The archetypal self in Swinburne's "Tristram of Lyonesse." *Psychocultural Review* 1:371–390.

Swinburne. A. C. 1904. *The Poems of Algernon Charles Swinburne.* 6 vols. New York: Harper.

_____. 1959–1962. *The Swinburne Letters.* Cecil Y. Lang, ed. 6 vols. New Haven: Yale University Press.

_____. 1970. *William Blake: A Critical Essay.* Hugh J. Luke, ed. Lincoln: University of Nebraska Press.

Thomas, Donald. 1979. *Swinburne: The Poet in His World.* New York: Oxford University Press.

Tredell, Nicolas. 1982. *Tristram of Lyonesse*: dangerous voyage. *Victorian Poetry* 20:97–111.

van Meurs, Jos. 1988. *Jungian Literary Criticism, 1920–1980: An Annotated, Critical Bibliography of Works in English (with a Selection of Titles after 1980).* Metuchen, N.J.: Scarecrow.

von Franz, Marie-Louise. 1964. The process of individuation. In *Man and His Symbols,* C. G. Jung, ed. Garden City, N.Y.: Doubleday.

_____. 1987. *On Dreams and Dying: A Jungian Interpretation.* Emmanuel Xipolitas Kennedy and Vernon Brooks, trans. Boston: Shambhala.

Woodberry, George Edward. 1905. *Swinburne.* New York: McClure, Phillips.

Chapter Four

A Jungian Analysis of Schizophrenia in Oscar Wilde's
The Picture of Dorian Gray

The nineteenth century dislike of Realism
is the rage of Caliban seeing his own face in a glass.
The nineteenth century dislike of Romanticism
is the rage of Caliban not seeing his own face in a glass.
Oscar Wilde, Preface to
The Picture of Dorian Gray

According to Jungian theory, visionary literature (literature stemming from the collective unconscious) compensates for contemporary psychic imbalance because such literature contains the "imagery of the collective unconscious" (Jung 1950, p. 93). Similar imagery can be found in dreams, fairy tales, and psychotic hallucinations; and in fact, Jung's work with schizophrenics led him to propose his theory of the collective unconscious (Storr 1983, p. 15). As I have pointed out elsewhere, Jung believes "it is a mistake to analyze a work of art strictly on the basis of the artist's biography or personal psychology, for if these ever fully explain the work of art, then it is reduced merely to a symptom . . . and is not worth further study" (Snider 1984, pp. 18–19; see also Jung 1950, p. 86). Whenever a large group of people become psychically imbalanced, "archetypal images [images from the collective unconscious] will appear in myths, in folk tales, and in more formal literature" (Snider 1984, p. 15). The compensatory images these forms offer may represent either positive or negative examples of contemporary one-sidedness, but they always propose to right the imbalance.

Richard Aldington is correct when he says, comparing *The Picture of Dorian Gray* with *Dr. Jekyll and Mr. Hyde*, that "the notion of dual personality was much in vogue at the time" Wilde wrote his novel; but Aldington is wrong when he asserts "there is only one character in the book — Oscar Wilde" (1946, p. 31). Of course there is much of Wilde himself in the book, as Wilde admitted (1962, p. 352); and the Marquess of Queensberry used *The Picture of Dorian Gray* to defend himself in Wilde's libel trial against him (Hyde 1975, pp. 133–134). Yet the novel is far from a case study of Wilde's personal psychology. In his story of the beautiful man who makes a Faustian bargain to stay forever young, Wilde reflects late Victorian psychic imbalance, an imbalance that was schizophrenic. Whatever else *The Picture of Dorian Gray* might say about Wilde and his aesthetic theories, it is an unconscious study of collective madness in late-nineteenth-century England.

The critics accorded *The Picture of Dorian Gray* a reception similar to that received by Swinburne's *Poems and Ballads* in the mid-1860s. As Martin Fido points out, "Wilde was beset by Philistines, proclaiming that he had written an immoral book" (1973, p. 85). The *Daily Chronicle* called the novel, as it appeared in *Lippincott's Monthly Magazine* (1890):

> a tale spawned from the leprous literature of the French *Décadents* — a poisonous book, the atmosphere of which is heavy with the mephitic odours of moral and spiritual putrefaction — a gloating study of the mental and physical corruption of a fresh, fair and golden youth. . . . Man is half angel and half ape, and Mr. Wilde's book has no real use if it be not to inculcate the "moral" that when you feel yourself becoming too angelic you cannot do better than rush out and make a beast of yourself. (Beckson 1970, p. 72)

In a letter dated June 30, 1890, Wilde responded immediately. From the "aesthetic point of view," he writes, it was "difficult to keep the moral in its proper secondary place; and even now I do not feel quite sure that I have been able to do so. I think the moral of the story is that all excess, as well as all renunciation, brings its punishment" (ibid.). Critics could not agree with Wilde because in his novel they found projected parts of their own collective, repressed unconscious, what Jung calls the shadow.

When the novel was published in book form, however, Wilde added six new chapters, as well as a preface, partly to soften some of the criticism (Hyde 1982, p. 138). His additions did little to still the negative comments. As Wilde's son, Vyvyan Holland, notes, "The English press was almost unanimous in its condemnation of the book" because, they claimed, "it was prurient, immoral, vicious, coarse, and crude. But the real reason for the attack was that it did so much to expose the hypocrisy of Victorian Englishmen who, living in one of the most vicious cities in the world, kept priding themselves, sanctimoniously, upon their virtue." Holland goes on to say that "London in the 1880s and 1890s was far more steeped in vice than Paris, at which England and the English Press kept pointing a finger of scorn" (1966, p. 70). Furthermore, as Fido writes, the critics' "unbalanced moral judgment emerged when they protested, not that Dorian Gray was shown to be a murderer and a blackmailer, but that it was distantly hinted that he might have been homosexual!" (1973, p. 85).

Richard Ellmann correctly asserts that "*Dorian Gray*, besides being about aestheticism, is also one of the first attempts to bring homosexuality into the English novel. Its appropriately covert presentation of this censored subject gave the book notoriety and originality" (1987, pp. 318–319). Ellmann also points out that Wilde named the protagonist of his novel after John Gray, an adored young man who was in all probability his lover from about 1889 to 1892 (ibid., pp. 307–308). That accounts for Dorian Gray's last name. Most likely Wilde chose the first name because of its connection with the ancient Greek Dorian states, where open homosexuality existed and was accepted, particularly in Sparta and Crete. Evidence for this fact exists in Plato's *Laws* (Dover 1978, p. 185); and as a classical scholar, Wilde no doubt was aware of the reputation of the Dorian states (Ellmann 1987, pp. 29–30, 60–61).

Late Victorian society was as unbalanced as the critics of *Dorian Gray*. What Jung said about the world since World War II, that it "has remained in a state of schizophrenia" (1964, p. 93), is equally true, albeit for other reasons, of the Victorian era, when virtually any reference to bodily functions was forbidden in so-called polite society. Victorian society had collectively repressed its shadow: "everything that the subject refuses to acknowledge about himself and yet is always thrusting itself upon him directly or indirectly" (Jung 1939, pp. 284–285). As Wendell Stacy Johnson points out, while publicly disapproving of nude paintings and statues, bowdlerizing the "bawdy parts of Chaucer and Shakespeare . . . and in general . . . [refusing] to say anything at all straight or simple about sex," the Victorian middle class actually shared with the other classes "an obsessive interest" in sex (1979, p. 6). Clearly, Victorian society was schizophrenic on the subject of sex.

Just as Dorian Gray himself projects his shadow onto his portrait, so did Wilde's critics project their collective shadow onto Wilde and his book. Like Caliban in the preface to the novel, they were enraged at what they saw in the looking glass of the novel because, without knowing it (or if they did know it they refused to acknowledge doing so), they saw their own faces. That Lord Queensberry should have used *The Picture of Dorian Gray* to support his accusation that Wilde was homosexual is not at all surprising: Queensberry, using Wilde as a scapegoat, was projecting his own shadow upon Wilde, just as, collectively, society was doing (Holland 1966, p. 104; see also Snider 1977, p. 225 and Perera 1986, p. 9). "Projections," as Jung writes, "change the world into the replica of one's own unknown face"; and projections account for the phenomenon of scapegoatism (Storr 1983, p. 92).

Whatever Wilde's fate has been in the academic community (and his reputation recovered long ago from his personal tragedy), he has remained particularly popular with the young.[1] Richard Ellmann notes that "the disrepute into which estheticism fell at the end of the nineteenth century did not lose Oscar Wilde his favorite audience of the young . . ." (1963, p. 342). And Edouard Roditi, who forty years ago had much to do with restoring Wilde's rightful place in literary history as a bridge between "established and aging Romanticism to what we now call modernism" asserts that Wilde continues to be "read by large numbers of adolescent or semi-literate readers" (1986, pp. 4–5). Obviously Wilde appeals to something in our collective psyche, even to this day.[2]

Although he cautions against a Freudian interpretation, wherein the artist is merely a "neurotic," Roditi suggests the following Freudian analysis of *Dorian Gray*:

> It might . . . be argued psychoanalytically that Dorian, Wilde's Id, is driven to self-inflicted death by his misinterpreting, in too selfishly literal a manner, the doctrines of beauty and pleasure which are preached by Lord Henry, Wilde's Ego; and that Basil, the author's Super-Ego, is killed when his warnings and reproaches might frustrate Dorian in his unbridled pursuit of sensual satisfactions. (1986, p. 124)

Roditi goes on:

> Taoists and Freudians alike would affirm that none of these three characters was right, or that all three are right in that rightness resides in achieving harmony among them, through self-knowledge, and in transcending, by contemplative inaction, the strife of their conflicting purposes. (Ibid.)

The point is, however, that harmony is not achieved, so that the novel reflects Victorian imbalance, not to mention the imbalance of our own age.

To Roditi, *The Picture of Dorian Gray* is "English literature's most perfect example of . . . the *Erziehungsroman* of dandyism" (ibid., p. 196). Roditi's interpretation is more Taoist than Freudian. For him,

> Lord Henry, Wilde's perfect dandy, expounds to Dorian a paradoxical philosophy of dandyism which shocks Basil Halward [sic] but appeals to the young narcissist. In the passion of his self-love, Dorian Gray distorts this doctrine and becomes a fallen dandy, corrupting all those who accompany him along his path and murdering his conscience, Basil Halward [sic]; finally, in self-inflicted death, Dorian meets the punishment of excessive self-love. (Ibid., p. 84)

Roditi continues,

> But Lord Henry's true doctrine . . .was a philosophy of inaction: beyond good and evil, for all his evil-sounding paradoxes which only illustrate the Taoist identity of contraries where both conscience and temptation are placed on the same footing but then transcended, Lord Henry never acts and never falls. (Ibid., pp. 84–85)

Writing some thirty years after Roditi, Donald H. Ericksen insists that *Dorian Gray's* "ethical message . . . must be based on Wilde's artistic credo," as stated in "The Critic as Artist": " 'life . . .has for its aim not *doing* but *being*, and not being merely, but *becoming*' " (Erickson 1977, p. 113). Lord Henry, Basil Hallward, and Sibyl Vane all fail to achieve "the aesthetic form that the proper critical spirit makes possible"; and Ericksen acknowledges that his own interpretation is close to Roditi's (ibid., pp. 113–114). Dorian Gray himself is a "true decadent," and his portrait

> becomes not the record of his sin or his conscience, but of his artistic decadence. When he ceases to be a spectator of life and becomes enmeshed in the mundane realities of self-gratification and crime, his life and personality cease to be art, and the suspension of time which is art's great gift finally ends. (Ibid., p. 115)

Valid as these interpretations are, they do not probe the deeper, psychological meaning of the novel. Philip K. Cohen comes closer to such a meaning when he observes that

> the commingling of art and life in this portrait [of Dorian Gray], the link between act and consequence, and the *disintegration of self resulting from split consciousness* become vigorously, unmistakeably manifest when Dorian stabs Basil's masterpiece. (1978, p. 148, italics mine)

For, as I have said, *The Picture of Dorian Gray* is in fact a study, a portrait as it were, of madness; and to understand its significance as visionary art, a Jungian interpretation is necessary.

A first reading of Dorian Gray's character suggests that he is a *puer aeternus*, an archetype mentioned by Jung and explored by Marie-Louise von Franz in her book, *Puer Aeternus*. As von Franz points out, the *puer aeternus* was an ancient god, mentioned in Ovid's *Metamorphoses*, a "god of divine youth, corresponding to such oriental gods as Tammuz, Attis, and Adonis." Von Franz uses the term "to indicate a certain type of young man who has an outstanding mother complex and who therefore behaves in certain typical ways" (1981, p. 1). He remains too long in adolescent psychology, retaining traits that are normal in a seventeen- or eighteen-year-old. Typically, he is either a homosexual or a Don Juan, and both terms could apply equally to Dorian Gray.[3] The *puer* has an "arrogant attitude . . . towards other people, due to both an inferiority complex and false feelings of superiority" (ibid., p. 2). He is never satisfied with any one job or woman (or man); he develops

> a form of neurosis which H. G. Baynes has described as the "provisional life"; that is, the strange attitude and feeling that the woman [in the case of a Don Juan] is *not yet* what is really wanted, and there is always the fantasy that sometime in the future the real thing will come about. If this attitude is prolonged, it means a constant inner refusal to commit oneself to the moment. (Ibid., p. 2)

Furthermore,

> *pueri aeterni* are generally very agreeable to talk with; they usually have interesting subjects to talk about and have an invigorating effect upon the listener; they do not like conventional situations . . . usually they are searching for genuine religion, a search that is typical for people in their late teens. Usually the youthful charm of the *puer aeternus* is prolonged through later stages of life. (Ibid., p. 4).

So far everything I've quoted about the *puer* seems to apply to Dorian Gray.[4] He is certainly an engaging personality, and he does take an interest in religion, albeit a superficial interest (Aldington 1946, pp. 296–297). Although his mother died when he was an infant, Dorian could have a mother complex in the sense that he seeks "the perfect woman who will give everything to a man and who is without any shortcomings" (von Franz 1981, p. 1). Lord Fermor tells Lord Henry that Dorian's mother was "an extraordinarily beautiful girl . . . one of the loveliest creatures I ever saw" (Aldington 1946, pp. 176–177). However, the man with a mother complex also seeks "the maternal woman who will enfold him in her arms and satisfy his every need" (von Franz 1981, p. 2). Dorian Gray rejects Sibyl Vane because she is a "complete failure" as an actress (Aldington 1946, p. 233), not because he wants a "maternal woman." To be sure, one of Dorian's great needs at the time is to have a woman who lives up to his aesthetic ideal, and Sibyl does not. Dorian Gray, in short, *is* a *puer aeternus*, but he is also mad — a psychopath. As von Franz shows, the two are not mutually exclusive (1981, p. 9).

Throughout the novel there are numerous references to madness. Due to a "mad passion," Dorian's mother had run away with his father, "a penniless young fellow, a mere nobody" who, as the mother was to do, died prematurely (Aldington 1946, pp. 178, 176). Dorian has a "mad adoration" for Sibyl Vane (ibid., p. 203). His Faustian bargain is described thus:

> He [Dorian Gray] had uttered a mad wish that he himself might remain young, and the portrait grow old; that his own beauty might be untarnished, and the face on the canvas bear the burden of his passions and his sins; that the painted image might be seared with the lines of suffering and thought, and that he might keep all the delicate bloom and loveliness of his then just conscious boyhood. (Ibid., p. 241)

Dorian has just rejected Sibyl Vane because she has failed to correspond to his image of her as a great actress. Instead, she has become an ordinary woman in love with him. Here his madness begins: "Suddenly there had fallen upon his brain that tiny scarlet speck that makes men mad" (ibid., p. 242).

Dorian Gray is at the point in his young life where he should be learning to accommodate the contrasexual — what Jung calls the anima — at its most elemental level, the primitive, symbolized by Sibyl Vane. Instead of accommodation, he succumbs to what von Franz calls the "malefic" aspect of the anima (1964 p. 178). Von Franz divides the stages of the anima into four: the "primitive woman," "romanticized beauty," "*eros* . . . spiritualized," and "wisdom" (ibid., p. 184–185). In order to become a whole person, what Jung calls individuated, a man must assimilate into his consciousness all four stages on the symbolic level. Dorian never gets beyond the first level and then only through projecting the image of the anima unto the women he meets and "ruins." Von Franz writes: "If the anima is lost out of sight, feeling is lost, and that happens often in schizophrenia" (1981, p. 283). In other words, by losing the anima "out of sight," Dorian has lost the "feminine" feeling function, the ability to "discriminate values" (ibid., p. 283).

Just before Dorian murders him, Basil Hallward declares: " 'You are mad, Dorian, or playing a part' " (Aldington 1946, p. 314). Basil is right. Dorian *is* mad. He has long been a paranoid schizophrenic, normal on the outside, mad inside. Jung's description of this kind of schizophrenia fits Dorian almost exactly:

> It consists in a simple doubling of the personality, which in milder cases is still held together by the identity of the two egos. The patient strikes us at first as completely normal . . . we suspect nothing. We converse normally with him, and at some point we let fall the word "Freemason." Suddenly the jovial face before us changes, a piercing look full of abysmal mistrust and inhuman fanaticism meets us from his eye. He has become a hunted, dangerous animal, surrounded by invisible enemies: the other ego has risen to the surface. (Storr 1983, pp. 40–41)

Jung could have been describing Dorian Gray just before he kills Basil:

> suddenly an uncontrollable feeling of hatred for Basil Hallward came over him, as though it had been suggested to him by the image on the canvas, whispered into his ear by those grinning lips. The mad passions of a hunted animal stirred within him, and he loathed the man who was seated at the table, more than in his whole life he had ever loathed anything. (Aldington 1946, pp. 317–318)

Jung's comments about a real-life schizophrenic whose love for his sister-in-law comes to naught could apply as well to Dorian Gray and his self-destroyed relationship with Sibyl Vane:

> His dream was destroyed, but this in itself would not have
> been harmful had it not also killed his feelings. For his intel-
> lect then took over the role of the brother and, with inquisi-
> torial sternness, destroyed every trace of feeling, holding
> before him the ideal of cold-blooded heartlessness. (Storr
> 1983, p. 42)

Instead of "brother," read "Lord Henry" and you have Dorian Gray,
whose feelings have been destroyed, who has become "cold-blooded" and
"heartless." Ruled by paranoia, he becomes "afraid" that if he leaves his
home for long "someone might gain access to the room" where he has
locked his incriminating portrait (Aldington 1946, p. 298). His secret life
"brawling with foreign sailors" and consorting "with thieves and coiners"
makes him all the more paranoiac (ibid., p. 299).

Dorian Gray also exhibits the "delusions and hallucinations" that are
classic symptoms of schizophrenia (Storr 1983, p. 40). Dorian

> used to wonder at the shallow psychology of those who con-
> ceive the Ego in man as a thing simple, permanent, reliable,
> and of one essence. To him, man was a being with myriad
> lives and myriad sensations, a complex multiform creature
> that bore within itself strange legacies of thought and pas-
> sion. (Aldington 1946, p. 300)

Dorian has delusions of grandeur:

> There were times when it appeared to Dorian Gray that the
> whole of history was merely the record of his own life, not as
> he had lived it in act and circumstance, but as his imagina-
> tion had created it for him, as it had been in his brain and in
> his passions. He felt he had known them all, those strange
> terrible figures that had passed across the stage of the world
> and made sin so marvellous and evil so full of subtlety. It
> seemed to him that in some mysterious way their lives had
> been his own. (Ibid., p. 302)

Dorian identifies with the malevolent historical figures whom "the hero of
the wonderful novel" Lord Henry had given him also identifies with; these
figures include such monsters as Caligula, Filippo, Duke of Milan, and
Gian Maria Visconti (ibid., pp. 302–303).[5]

In his essay, "On the Psychogenesis of Schizophrenia," Jung recalls being "amazed at the number of schizophrenics whom we almost never see in psychiatric hospitals. These cases are partially camouflaged as obsessional neuroses, compulsions, phobias, and hysterias, and they are very careful never to go near an asylum" (quoted in Storr 1983, p. 43). When we consider Dorian Gray's obsession with his hidden portrait, when we consider his compulsions to fly to the opium dens, his fear of growing old, and his hysterical actions (murder, for instance), what Jung has to say about schizophrenics again applies to Dorian Gray, who never goes "near an asylum."

Elsewhere I have maintained that *The Picture of Dorian Gray* is a case of shadow projection (Snider 1977, p. 225). Jung, I should emphasize, says "one meets with projections, one does not make them" (Storr 1983, p. 92). Carried to the extreme, shadow projection can result in madness and suicide, as it does in *Dorian Gray*, where Dorian actually becomes possessed by negative shadow traits, traits that have gone beyond the personal shadow to the collective, as his obsession with the malevolent historical figures I have cited shows.

But the portrait is not the only shadow projection in the novel. All archetypes have a positive as well as a negative side; and the shadow, although usually associated with the evil side of the psyche, is no exception. Since the shadow is personified in a figure of the same sex, Basil Hallward is to Dorian Gray a projection of the positive shadow. The fact that the former seems to have a sexual attraction to the latter is further corroboration that together Basil and Dorian might have achieved a psychic whole. But Dorian rejects the wholeness Basil offers. Early in the novel, before Dorian comes under Lord Henry's influence, Basil tells Lord Henry: "The harmony of soul and body — how much that is! We in our madness have separated the two, and have invented a realism that is vulgar, an ideality that is void" (Aldington 1946, p. 150). Although Basil refers to art and "the perfection of the spirit that is Greek," his declaration accurately describes the psychic split of the age and foreshadows Dorian Gray's psychic split which leads to a madness that destroys him (ibid., p. 150).

Richard Ellmann believes Dorian's "violent action is not to destroy himself but to get rid of his picture. It is only the image which he means to attack, and his own death is a side-effect and an unintended one" (1963, p. 355). Perhaps Dorian does not intend to kill himself, yet his entire adult life has been self-destructive and compulsively so. The portrait is a concrete representation, a projection, of the repressed side of his psyche, his second ego, which has lately impinged itself upon his "respectable" ego so that he wildly makes efforts to come to terms with his shadow. This is why he tries to do right by Hetty Merton. Jung says of schizophrenics that

> as reality loses its hold, the determining power of the inner world increases. This process leads up to a climax when the patient suddenly becomes more or less conscious of his disso-ciation from reality: in a sort of panic he begins making pathological efforts to get back to his environment. (Jung 1952, p. 40)

When Dorian, loathing his own still beautiful physical appearance, shat-ters the "curiously carved mirror . . . Lord Henry had given to him, so many years ago," he begins to realize that although he is conscious of his "dissociation from reality," he is not going to change (Aldington 1946, p. 387). The portrait, "this mirror of his soul," confirms this, and when he attacks it with the knife he used to kill Basil Hallward, he is really attack-ing himself, just as he was when he murdered Basil (ibid., p. 390). His physical self-destruction is simply the confirmation, the inevitable result, of his psychic suicide.

Of the novel's major characters, we are left with Lord Henry, who deliberately sets out to "dominate" Dorian Gray with his own ideas and "temperament": "to hear one's own intellectual views echoed back to one with all the added music of passion and youth" (ibid., pp. 179, 180). Almost every critic who comments on *The Picture of Dorian Gray* identi-fies Lord Henry as Mephistopheles to Dorian's Faust. I do not argue with this position; yet I tend to agree with Roditi that Lord Henry's doctrines should have been positive had Dorian understood them rightly.

Archetypally, then, who or what does Lord Henry represent? Again, I emphasize the fact that archetypes have two sides, positive and negative. As Jung says in *The Archetypes and the Collective Unconscious*,

> It is an essential characteristic of psychic figures that they are duplex or at least capable of duplication; at all events they are bipolar and oscillate between their positive and negative meanings. Thus the "supraordinate" personality can appear in a despicable and distorted form, like for instance Mephistopheles, who is really more positive as a personality than the vapid and unthinking careerist Faust. (1951, p. 183)

Applied to *Dorian Gray*, this means that Lord Henry could have been a positive influence — even more; as a "supraordinate" personality for Dorian, he could have been an image of the Self or psychic wholeness. Whereas Basil was, symbolically, a part of Dorian, his positive shadow, Lord Henry, were Dorian Gray psychically capable of growth, should have been an image of wholeness, a Wise Old Man. Sadly, for Dorian Gray, Lord Henry symbolized quite the opposite.

The tragedy is that in the case of Dorian Gray, as with so many schizophrenics, a cure was not possible (see Storr 1983, p. 43). He had become overwhelmed by unconscious forces he could no longer control. If what happened to the author of *The Picture of Dorian Gray* is any indicator, late Victorian society itself never accommodated its own collective shadow, and to this day the collective psychic split has never been healed.

Notes

1. Oscar Wilde's scholarly rehabilitation took a long time, however. As Edouard Roditi notes, "Wilde's . . . writings remained practically taboo for a number of decades [after his trials in the mid-1890s] as subjects of serious critical discussion, while his immensely popular and financially successful comedies were immediately withdrawn from the London stage" (1986, p. 153).

2. Evidence from my own students, the several film versions of *The Picture of Dorian Gray* and the frequent and popular revivals of Wilde's plays (especially *The Importance of Being Earnest*), seem to corroborate this opinion, although I have no scientific surveys to offer. In a recent essay, "Allegorical Performance in *Dorian Gray*," Donald L. Lawler, also citing Jung, recognizes "the powerful appeal this archetype [of Dorian Gray] has had for the modern imagination as both a touchstone of popular culture and a subject of critical inquiry" (1988, p. 452).

3. Von Franz calls homosexuality a "disturbance" and a "problem," although she admits that "Jung . . . [thought] perhaps . . . [homosexuality] is an unconscious compensation for overpopulation . . . so a certain number of people refrain from producing children" (1981, p. 9). In a letter to Freud, Jung said: "Removal of the moral stigma from homosexuality as a method of contraception is a cause to be promoted with the utmost energy." However, Jung refers to those homosexuals as "inferior men" who are "now forced into marriage," thus presumably "producing children." Jung adds: "Because of our shortsightedness we fail to recognize the biological services rendered by homosexual seducers. Actually they should be credited with something of the sanctity of monks" (McGuire 1974, p. 298). A discussion of this passage, together with a reference to Jung's "own homosexual assault as a boy, and his relationship with Freud," in Vincent Brome's *Jung: Man and Myth* (1978, pp. 121–122), is apparently the basis for Colin Wilson's statement that "Jung's biographer Vincent Brome suggests that Jung was aware of a streak of homosexuality in his own makeup" (1984, p. 46). Despite Jung's apparent tolerance, he nevertheless greatly oversimplifies the subject and betrays the homophobia common at the time. Jung never examined the topic of homosexuality in depth (see Hopcke 1988). Jungian analysts today recognize, as Anthony Stevens says, that "the homosexual relationship, like its heterosexual counterpart, is a perfectly valid way of working out the individuation process" (1982, p. 198). Robert H. Hopcke, in his recently published book, *Jung, Jungians, and Homosexuality*, for the first time posits in depth a Jungian theory of homosexuality, a theory that is "archetypally based, empirically supportable, psychologically profound, and spiritually evocative" (1989, p. 9).

4. Lawler notes: "Dorian is himself an idealization of youthful beauty" (1988, p. 441).

5. Jung calls such identification psychic "inflation" (Jung 1953, p. 157).

Works Cited

Aldington, Richard, ed. 1946. *The Portable Oscar Wilde*. New York: Viking.

Beckson, Karl, ed. 1970. *Oscar Wilde: The Critical Heritage*. New York: Barnes.

Brome, Vincent. 1978. *Jung: Man and Myth*. London: Granada.

Cohen, Philip K. 1978. *The Moral Vision of Oscar Wilde*. Rutherford, N.J.: Fairleigh Dickinson University Press.

Dover, K. J. 1978. *Greek Homosexuality*. London: Duckworth.

Ellmann, Richard. 1963. Romantic pantomime in Oscar Wilde. *Partisan Review* 30:342–355.

_____. 1987. *Oscar Wilde*. New York: Knopf.

Ericksen, Donald H. 1977. *Oscar Wilde*. Boston: Twayne.

Fido, Martin. 1973. *Oscar Wilde*. New York: Viking.

Holland, Vyvyan. 1966. *Oscar Wilde and His World*. Revised ed. London: Thames and Hudson.

Hopcke, Robert H. 1988. Jung and homosexuality: a clearer vision. *Journal of Analytical Psychology* 33:65–80.

_____. 1989. *Jung, Jungians, and Homosexuality*. Boston: Shambhala.

Hyde, H. Montgomery, ed. 1975. *Oscar Wilde: A Biography*. New York: Farrar.

_____. 1982. *The Annotated Oscar Wilde: Poems, Fiction, Plays, Lectures, Essays, and Letters*. New York: Clarkson N. Potter.

Johnson, Wendell Stacy. 1979. *Living in Sin: The Victorian Sexual Revolution*. Chicago: Nelson-Hall.

Jung, C. G. 1939. Conscious, unconscious, and individuation. *CW* 9i:275–289. Princeton, N.J.: Princeton University Press, 1959.

_____. 1950. Psychology and literature. *CW* 15:84–107. Princeton, N.J.: Princeton University Press, 1966.

_____. 1951. The psychological aspects of Kore. *CW* 9i:182–205. Princeton, N.J.: Princeton University Press, 1959.

_____. 1952. *Symbols of Transformation: An Analysis of the Prelude to a Case of Schizophrenia*. *CW*, vol. 5. Princeton: N.J.: Princeton University Press, 1967.

_____. 1953. *Two Essays on Analytical Psychology*. R. F. C. Hull, trans. New York: World.

Jung, C. G., et al. 1964. *Man and His Symbols*. Garden City, N.Y.: Doubleday.

Lawler, Donald L., ed. 1988. *The Picture of Dorian Gray: A Norton Critical Edition*. New York: Norton.

McGuire, William, ed. 1974. *The Freud/Jung Letters: The Correspondence Between Sigmund Freud and C. G. Jung.* Ralph Manheim and R. F. C. Hull, trans. Princeton, N.J.: Princeton University Press.

Perera, Sylvia Brinton. 1986. *The Scapegoat Complex: Toward a Mythology of Shadow and Guilt.* Toronto: Inner City.

Roditi, Edouard. 1986. *Oscar Wilde.* Revised ed. New York: New Directions.

Snider, Clifton. 1977. C. G. Jung's analytical psychology and literary criticism. *Psychocultural Review* 1:96–108; 216–242.

———. 1984. Jungian theory, its literary application, and a discussion of *The Member of the Wedding.* In *Psychological Perspectives on Literature: Freudian Dissidents and Non-Freudians, A Casebook*, Joseph Natoli, ed. Hamden, Conn.: Archon.

Stevens, Anthony. 1982. *Archetypes: A Natural History of the Self.* New York: Quill.

Storr, Anthony, ed. 1983. *The Essential Jung.* Princeton, N.J.: Princeton University Press.

von Franz, Marie-Louise. 1981. *Puer Aeternus.* 2nd ed. Santa Monica, Calif.: Sigo.

———. 1964. The process of individuation. In *Man and His Symbols*, C. G. Jung, ed. Garden City, N.Y.: Doubleday, pp. 158–229.

Wilde, Oscar. 1962. *The Letters of Oscar Wilde.* Rupert Hart-Davis, ed. New York: Harcourt.

Wilson, Colin. 1984. *C. G. Jung: Lord of the Underworld.* Wellingborough, England: Aquarian.

Chapter Five

Androgyny in Virginia Woolf:
Jungian Interpretations of *Orlando*
and *The Waves**

So she was now darkened, stilled,
and become, with the addition of this Orlando,
what is called, rightly or wrongly,
a single self, a real self.

Virginia Woolf,
Orlando: A Biography

I

Apart from Bernard in *The Waves* (1931), the character in the fiction of Virginia Woolf who probably best exemplifies her idea of the androgynous — and, therefore, whole — personality is Orlando. Because her ideas about androgyny and the individual, especially the creative individual, are so close to those of Jung, it seems odd that no extensive Jungian study has been made of *Orlando: A Biography* (1928). In *Virginia Woolf and the Androgynous Vision*, Nancy Topping Bazin points out the similarity between the theories of Woolf and Jung, but Bazin refers to *Orlando* only thrice, preferring to examine the other novels, presumably because *Orlando*, as a "fantasy-biography," is not so serious a piece of literature as Woolf's other work (1973, p. 139).[1]

In what generic category to place *Orlando* has always been a problem. Conrad Aiken, reviewing the book for the February 1929 issue of *Dial*, writes that the critics "have not known quite how to take it [*Orlando*] — whether to regard it as a biography, or a satire on biography; as a history, or a satire on history; as a novel, or as an allegory" (quoted in Majumbar

---

*Portions of this chapter were first published as " 'A Single Self': A Jungian Interpretation of Virginia Woolf's *Orlando*" in *Modern Fiction Studies*, © 1979 by Purdue Research Foundation, West Lafayette, Indiana 47907. Reprinted with permission.

and McLaurin, pp. 147–149). Joanne Trautmann writes that "among other categories, it may be seen as a parody of biography, an essay in the exotic, a mock-heroic novel of ideas, an imaginative literary and social history of England, and a biography of V. Sackville-West" (1973, p. 40). Trautmann also points out that *Orlando* "has been critically analyzed from several angles, as it requires" (ibid.). I propose to analyze the book from a Jungian point of view because the writing of *Orlando* and the book itself illustrate a number of Jungian theories. The process of writing the book is a fine example of Jung's theory of creativity. The book itself shows the individuation of the character Orlando, how that character is able to develop each of Jung's four functions of consciousness and then to achieve an integrated personality (what Jung calls the Self) through the joining of the anima and the animus.

Also analyzed here is *The Waves*, perhaps Virginia Woolf's finest and certainly her most experimental novel. The composition of *The Waves*, far more arduous than was the writing of *Orlando*, also illustrates Jung's theory of creativity as well as Woolf's own ideas about the androgynous writer as articulated in *A Room of One's Own* (1929). A poetic novel without conventional plot, *The Waves* shows its seven characters gradually and mystically coalescing into one character, Bernard, Virginia's Woolf's most androgynous character.

As I have shown elsewhere, Jung's theory of creativity echoes Platonic ideas (Chapter One, p. 6, and Snider 1977, pp. 104–105). Jung writes: "The unborn work in the psyche of the artist is a force of nature that achieves its end either with tyrannical might or with the subtle cunning of nature herself, quite regardless of the personal fate of the man who is its vehicle" (1931, p. 75). Jung echoes the romantic idea that the artist is compelled to create: "Art is a kind of innate drive that seizes a human being and makes him its instrument" (1950, p. 101).[2] For Jung, as for the romantics, the artist is, as it were, an Eolian lyre upon which the winds of inspiration play. The work of art springs from the unconscious by means of an "autonomous complex" (Jung 1931, p. 75).[3] In other words, the artist cannot help but create.

The composition of *Orlando* seems to correspond exactly to Jung's neo-Platonic theory. In a letter dated October 9, 1927, to Sackville-West, Woolf describes how she began to write *Orlando*. She had been unable to "screw a word" for another book she was working on. Then "[I] at last dropped my head in my hands; dipped my pen in the ink, and wrote these words, as if automatically, on a clean sheet: Orlando: A Biography. No sooner had I done this than my body was flooded with rapture and my brain with ideas. I wrote till 12." In another letter to Sackville-West, dated October 13–14, 1927, Woolf writes: "I am writing at great speed. For the third time I begin a sentence, [sic] The truth is I'm so engulfed in Orlando I can think of nothing else" (Nicolson and Trautmann, vol. 3, pp. 428, 430).[4] If any more evidence is required to show that *Orlando* was written in a spontaneous fashion that corresponds exactly to Jung's theory of creativity, I need only to quote from the entry in Virginia Woolf's diary dated December 20, 1927: "How extraordinarily unwilled by me but potent in its own right by the way Orlando was! as if it shoved everything aside to come into existence" (Bell 1977–1984, vol. 3, p. 168). Of course, it would be foolish to claim that *Orlando* sprang wholly from Woolf's unconscious. She researched her subjects, Knole House and the Sackvilles; and she drew on personal experience and observation. She consciously made *Orlando* a monument to the woman she had loved physically and whom she continued to love spiritually the rest of her life. As Nigel Nicolson writes: "It [*Orlando*] was her most elaborate love-letter, rendering Vita androgynous and immortal: it transformed her story into a myth, gave her back to Knole. Without shame on either side, she identified Vita as her model by the dedication and the photographs" (Nicolson and Trautmann 1975–1980, vol. 3, p. xxii).

To the extent that *Orlando* draws on what Jung terms the collective unconscious, in its use of archetypal patterns and symbols, *Orlando* is a myth for the twentieth century. As far as we know, Virginia Woolf never read Jung or Freud and was aware of their ideas only from what she heard in conversation (see Richter 1970, pp. 63–64), but if this is the case, it makes *Orlando* all the more extraordinary. It is her most lighthearted book, and it indicates that, as an artist, Woolf has learned to laugh — the problem that so concerns Hermann Hesse's *Steppenwolf*, a novel informed by Jungian ideas.[5]

For a writer to be balanced, he or she should have both humor and seriousness. Psychic balance is the great aim of Jungian analytical psychology, and that is why Orlando, apart from Bernard, seems the most psychically whole of the characters of Virginia Woolf. At times, Orlando can be the most extreme kind of introvert, as when he withdraws into himself after Nicholas Greene betrays him by writing a satire on "a noble Lord at home." Orlando "felt that if he need never speak to another man or woman so long as he lived . . . he might make out what years remained to him in tolerable content" (Woolf 1928, pp. 95, 97). At other times Orlando manages to behave as an extravert, as when he is the ambassador to Constantinople. On the whole, however, he/she is at heart an introvert who treasures his/her solitude.

In his psychology of the conscious mind, Jung calls introversion and extraversion psychological types. In addition to these are the four functions of consciousness: sensation, thinking, feeling, and intuition. Most people are able to develop one or two of these functions to a high degree, but Orlando, by the end of her "biography," has been able to develop all four functions of consciousness.

The sensation type of individual perceives the world through conscious senses. Early in the novel, as a boy of sixteen, Orlando has already developed this function: "He loved . . . to feel the earth's spine beneath him." Emersed in nature, he feels "as if all the fertility and amorous activity of a summer's evening were woven web-like about his body" (ibid., p. 19). The "earth's spine" is "the hard root of the oak tree." "The Oak Tree" is the title of the poem Orlando works on for some three hundred years, and, as we shall see, it is symbolic of Orlando's psyche. As it grows, so does Orlando.

Orlando, as a poet and man — and later woman — of letters, must be able to think: to, in the words of Jolande Jacobi, "apprehend the world and adjust to it by way of thought or cognition" (1968, p. 12). And think Orlando assuredly does: for "months and years of his life," he ponders such questions as "What is love? What friendship? What truth?" (Woolf 1928, p. 99).

Traditionally, the thinking and sensation functions have been placed in the sphere of "masculine" activities, and it is no accident, I think, that it is as a male that Orlando develops these functions. When he becomes a woman, at the age of thirty, he develops the more traditionally "feminine" functions: feeling and intuition. As Trautmann observes: "At thirty Orlando is just beginning to operate fully, since until that time she has known only half of the complete, androgynous human nature" (1973, p. 45).

Feeling, in the Jungian usage of the word, has nothing to do with the sense of touch. It is, rather, "a kind of *judgment*, differing from intellectual judgment in that its aim is not to establish conceptual relations but to set up a subjective criterion of acceptance or rejection" (Jung 1921, p. 434). As a woman among the gypsies, Orlando is able to look at "the red hyacinth, the purple iris . . . [and] to cry out in ecstasy at the goodness, the beauty of nature" (Woolf 1928, pp. 143–144). The gypsies are unable to share her feelings, which are judgments based on "a subjective criterion of acceptance."

The intuition function is perhaps the hardest to understand or to develop. Orlando is, nevertheless, able near the end of the novel to perceive the world intuitively, that is, through the unconscious. When she meets an older gentleman in the Victorian Age, she intuitively recognizes him as Nicholas Greene:

> "Sir Nicholas!" she replied. For she was made aware intuitively by something in his bearing that the scurrilous penny-a-liner, who had lampooned her and many another in the time of Queen Elizabeth, was now risen in the world and become certainly a knight and doubtless a dozen other fine things into the bargain. (Ibid., p. 276)

A few pages earlier she had intuitively learned that her future husband, Marmaduke Bonthrop Shelmerdine, spends most of his time voyaging around Cape Horn and that he is actually a woman, just as he recognizes her as a man (ibid., p. 252).

Before reaching the wholeness symbolized by the uniting of the opposites of anima/animus (or the ego with the contrasexual), the individual must accommodate the shadow—the repressed, often unacknowledged and negative, parts of the psyche, always symbolized by a member of one's own sex. *Orlando* opens with an image of male destructiveness: Orlando, a sixteen-year-old youth, is "slicing at the head of a Moor which swung from the rafters," a head "Orlando's father, or perhaps his grandfather, had struck . . . from the shoulders of a vast Pagan" (ibid., p. 13). The "blade" with which he attacks the head is a masculine symbol, and we have here Orlando acting out the shadow side of his psyche.

Virginia Woolf makes clear early on that *Orlando* is about opposing parts of the psyche: "in truth, his [Orlando's] mind was . . . a welter of opposites" (ibid., p. 22). As a man, he is "adored of many women and some men" (ibid., p. 125). When Orlando becomes a woman, "it was still a woman she loved; and if the consciousness of being of the same sex had any effect at all, it was to quicken and deepen those feelings which she had had as a man." She has, in other words, a heightened consciousness, an understanding of "a thousand hints and mysteries" about "the obscurity" that "divides the sexes" (ibid., p. 161). the Archduchess Harriet, really a man who had fallen in love with the male Orlando and therefore dressed as a woman in order to meet him, is symbolic of the shadow, also, for Orlando. Harriet/Harry symbolizes some less attractive characteristics of the male—acquisitiveness (money and property—he has "something like twenty million ducats in a strong box . . . [and] more acres than any nobleman in England" (ibid., p. 180)), love of hunting for sport, a weakness for gambling (he was a "born gambler" (ibid., p. 182)). Orlando is now mature enough psychically to reject these undesirable shadow traits as objectified in a suitor she does not love.

Ironically, Orlando does not fully realize the shadow until he becomes a woman and experiences the way women are treated by men in a male-dominated society. Eventually, she learns to enjoy "the love of both sexes equally" (ibid., p. 221), so that homosexuality, or bisexuality, is symbolic of wholeness for her. Orlando has now accommodated the shadow and approached a level of psychological wholeness that perhaps can best be explained by the archetypal symbols that Virginia Woolf employs.

Apart from the two most important and integrally related symbols, the house and the oak tree, which run throughout and unite the novel, a cluster of other symbols suggests that the novel is about individuation, the "religious" process through which the person reaches Selfhood or psychic wholeness. Maud Bodkin has identified these symbols as the poet (Shakespeare, and I would include Nick Greene), the sea captain (Shelmerdine, and I would add the captain who first introduces the feminine Orlando to Western masculine-dominated society), and the wild goose that appears at the very end of the novel. These figures are, for Orlando the woman, the animus. Her former gender has introduced her to the earlier stages of the animus, the physical and romantic stages. The animus as symbolized by the poet–captain–wild goose provides her with what Bodkin calls "a way of approach to Reality, or to the Divine" (1934, p. 307).[6] Having experienced the anima, with Sasha and other women and as a woman herself, Orlando symbolizes the joining the anima/animus. She has experienced the contrasexual, male and female, in her own body and psyche, and, therefore, at the end of the novel she is "a single self, a real self" (Woolf 1928, p. 314), and she is "one and entire" (ibid., p. 320). No one is ever fully individuated in life, but Orlando reaches Selfhood for the first time in her life and stands with Bernard as Woolf's most androgynous character.

This is reinforced by the two symbols that unite the novel: the house and the oak tree. It was a dream about a large house that first gave Jung his conception of the collective unconscious. Like Knole, the house about which Woolf is writing, Jung's house has stood for centuries and symbolizes history. The top story begins in the rococo era, and as one proceeds down the stairs, one goes back into history until one is in prehistoric times (Jung 1963, pp. 158–159). While Knole does not date from prehistoric times, it is thought that its foundations date from Roman times (Sackville-West 1947, p. 5). Woolf clearly intends that the house should stand for the history of the Sackvilles and of England and its literature. Unconsciously, however, she has created a symbol that stands for the psyche of her heroine. The roots of the psyche reach into the unknown, into the collective unconscious. The branches are in the open air of the known, the conscious. And as Knole grows, as Orlando furnishes it, so grows the psyche of Orlando.

"The Oak Tree," the poem and the actual tree itself, is perhaps the most important symbol, apart from Orlando herself, in the novel. Based on Sackville-West's prize-winning poem, "The Land," it is the only piece of her writing Orlando preserves throughout the centuries. As a work of art, it is a product of the unconscious shaped by the conscious mind. As a tree, it stands for the *coniunctio*, the joining of opposites. Like the house itself, its roots go down to the collective unconscious, and its branches breathe the air of consciousness. J. E. Cirlot points out that Jung maintains that the tree "has a symbolic, bisexual nature, as can be seen in the fact that, in Latin, the endings of the names of trees are masculine even though their gender is feminine" (1962, p. 331). The successful completion of the poem symbolizes that Orlando has, for the time being, reached that union of opposites, of anima/animus, of the Self. Because of this fusion of the contrasexual she has become androgynous, her mind and her psyche, to use Woolf's own words, "fully fertilised," able to use "all its faculties" (1929, p. 171).

II

The words I have just quoted from *A Room of One's Own* (1929) come from a passage where Virginia Woolf proposes ideas remarkably similar to those of Carl Jung. She asks "whether there are two sexes in the mind corresponding to the two sexes in the body, and whether they also require to be united in order to get complete satisfaction and happiness?" She goes on

> amateurishly to sketch a plan of the soul so that in each of us two powers preside, one male, one female; and in the man's brain, the man predominates over the woman, and in the woman's brain, the woman predominates over the man. The normal and comfortable state of being is that when the two live in harmony together, spiritually co-operating. If one is a man, still the woman part of the brain must have effect; and a woman also must have intercourse with the man in her. Coleridge perhaps meant this when he said that a great mind is androgynous. (1929, p. 170)

Then Woolf goes on to declare: "It is when this fusion takes place that the mind is fully fertilised and uses all its faculties. Perhaps a mind that is purely masculine cannot create, any more than a mind that is purely feminine" (ibid., pp. 170–171). She speculates that Coleridge "meant, perhaps, that the androgynous mind is resonant and porous; that it transmits emotion without impediment; that it is naturally creative, incandescent and undivided" (ibid., p. 171).

A little later Woolf decides

> that it is fatal for any one who writes to think of their sex. It is fatal to be a man or woman pure and simple; one must be woman-manly or man-womanly. . . .Some collaboration has to take place in the mind between the woman and the man before the act of creation can be accomplished. Some marriage of opposites has to be consummated. (Ibid., p. 181)

She cites Shakespeare as an example of the androgynous writer, and adds "Keats and Sterne and Cowper and Lamb and Coleridge" (ibid., p. 180). Clearly, of all the arts, great writing requires two functions, one characteristically masculine, the thinking function, the other characteristically feminine, the intuition function. Putting it another way, writing requires making logical, cognitive forms or structures; it requires conscious shaping. Imaginative writing also requires jumping beyond logic to make connections hitherto unthought of, to create images and symbols that derive from the unconscious. Showing the development of all four functions of consciousness in one character who lives over three hundred years and changes sexes, showing the connections between anima/animus in *Orlando* and their final fusion into the Self, showing in *The Waves* how one personality can form from six or seven various characters with all their male and female traits — this is writing androgynously. And the writing of these two novels exemplifies the kind of androgynous writing Virginia Woolf talks about in *A Room of One's Own*.[7]

The Waves (1931) was not composed with the same rush of inspiration as *Orlando*. For the most part, the work was painstaking, and it took two years and two full manuscripts to write (Nicolson and Trautmann 1975–1980, vol. 4, p. xx). She recorded in her diary (March 1, 1930): "If ever a book drained me, this one [*The Waves*] does" (Bell 1977–1984, vol. 3, p. 295). Consciously, she aimed for "a saturated, unchopped, completeness" in this novel (ibid., vol. 3, p. 343). Yet with all her conscious effort, she could record (on February 7, 1931) finishing the last ten pages thus:

I wrote the words O Death fifteen minutes ago, having reeled across the last ten pages with some moments of such intensity & intoxication that I seemed only to stumble after my own voice, or almost, after some sort of speaker (as when I was mad). I was almost afraid, remembering the voices that used to fly ahead. (Ibid., vol. 4, p. 10)

This was a time when, as Leonard Woolf writes in *Downhill All the Way*, "genius or inspiration seemed to take control . . . in . . . [a] kind of emotional and imaginative volcanic eruption" (1960–1969, pp. 53–54). Her husband felt that when Virginia Woolf wrote any of her novels (or the first drafts of them) she was in a similar "psychological state": "The tension was great and unremitting; it was emotionally volcanic; the conscious mind, though intent, seemed to follow a hair's breadth behind the voice, or the 'thought,' which flew ahead" (ibid., p. 54). At least, Leonard thought, this was her state when she wrote out her drafts in the morning by hand. Later in the day, when she rewrote the morning's work out on a typewriter, "The conscious, critical intellect was in control and the tension was less." So much was the difference between her writing fiction and criticism that at lunch, Leonard writes, "I could tell by the depth of the flush on her face whether she had been writing fiction or criticism" (ibid., p. 54).

None of this contradicts Jung's ideas about creativity. Even in the most inspired work, a conscious shaping must take place. It is relevant that Virginia Woolf should refer to her madness and her hearing of voices when she records her finishing *The Waves*; for, as I pointed out in my chapter on *The Picture of Dorian Gray*, symbols from the collective unconscious appear in the hallucinations of the mad as well as in visionary literature. As Jung writes, "psychotic products often contain a wealth of meaning such as is ordinarily found only in the works of genius" (1950, p. 92), and *The Waves* is, I feel, a work of genius. Leonard Woolf is not alone in calling *The Waves* "the best of all her books" (1960–1969, p. 148). He told his wife it was a "masterpiece" (Bell 1977–1984, vol. 4, p. 36), and it is. It is a masterpiece of visionary art, one in which she gives us the most complete, the most androgynous, the most individuated of her characters — Bernard.

That so much has been written about *The Waves* (indeed, about Virginia Woolf herself, both her life and her work) indicates the collective, compensatory appeal of her work.[8] One critic calls *The Waves* "an accomplishment unmatched by . . . [Woolf's] other novels" (Gorsky 1978, p. 198). Eric Warner, who devotes an entire book to *The Waves*, calls it

"Virginia Woolf's most formidable and challenging work of art" (1987, p. xiv). Phyllis Rose calls *The Waves* Woolf's "most ambitious novel" (1978, p. 16), one which "confirmed her reputation as an experimental writer," but Rose seems not much to like *The Waves*: "it is a much less vital book than *To the Lighthouse*," she writes (ibid., p. 196). As with *Orlando*, there is a debate over what generic category to put *The Waves* into, over "whether or not . . . [*The Waves*] can be called a novel" (Warner 1987, p. 1). Critics note the poetry of Woolf's prose and the fact that *The Waves* lacks conventional plot; however, to summarize the criticism here any further would be superfluous. I shall try to stay with my approach, which I hope will make this difficult novel lucid, at least from the viewpoint of Jung's analytical psychology.

Louis says, early in the novel, "I seem . . .to have lived many thousand years" (1931, p. 66); and he is the one who hears the "chained beast" (ibid., p. 67), the "elephant" (ibid., p. 10) stamping on the shore. The outsider, the Australian "alien, external" (ibid., p. 94), he understands that his "roots go down through veins of lead and silver, through damp, marshy places that exhale odours to a knot made of oak roots bound together in the centre" (ibid., p. 95). Intuitively, perhaps because of his position as an outsider which forces him to internalize, he understands the primal origins of the personality — the archetypal roots. Like the oak tree in *Orlando*, the allusion to "oak roots" here foreshadows wholeness, for they are "bound together in the centre"; and like all the other characters, Louis is part of Bernard's personality. They are all projections of archetypal symbols already within his psyche, where, he realizes, "There are many rooms — many Bernards" (ibid., p. 260). These symbolic characters are together a cluster of symbols needing to come together to make a whole. Although Bernard marries and becomes a father, he never projects onto his wife and child with anything like the same intensity the symbols he projects onto these friends.

Bernard intuits this identification with his friends early on: "I do not believe in separation," he says. "We are not single" (ibid., p. 67). Harvena Richter has diagrammed Bernard's "complete androgynous personality" in the "mental realm" and in the "physical realm." In the former, Bernard represents "language" as a "story-teller and phrase-maker." Neville is the "conscious," representing the "ordering power of the mind"; Louis is "memory, history and time"; Percival, "spirit, sun, light." On the feminine side, Susan is the "creative feminine principle"; Jinny, "creative energy, fire and motion"; and Rhoda, the "unconscious, the dreaming imagination" (Richter 1970, p. 247). In the "physical realm," Susan is the "normal mother figure"; Jinny, "feminine sexuality"; and Rhoda, "fear of flesh."

Percival, bridging the male–female sides here as in the mental realm, is the "life-force"; Louis, "fear of flesh"; Neville, "homosexuality"; and Bernard the "normal father figure" (ibid., p. 248). It takes all these opposites and seeming contradictions to make a whole, so that Bernard can say near the end of the novel: "I am not one person; I am many people; I do not altogether know who I am — Jinny, Susan, Neville, Rhoda, or Louis: or how to distinguish my life from theirs" (Woolf 1931, p. 276).[9] He is experiencing a mystical union such as only an individuated person feels. And, as in *Tristram of Lyonesse*, this union, this "mystic sense of completion" is accompanied by music: "a painful, guttural, visceral, also soaring, lark-like, pealing song" (ibid., pp. 250–251). The music comes from the unconscious (the "visceral") and unites it (the unconscious), "lark-like," with the conscious. As in Tristram and Iseult and as in Orlando, the psychic opposites of anima/animus and of unconscious/conscious are united in Bernard.

This unity has not come about easily. First Bernard had to realize the differences in each of the others. Separation from primal unity involves suffering; achieving wholeness requires great struggle. "But we were all different," he says:

> The wax — the virginal wax that coats the spine melted in different patches for each of us. The growl of the boot-boy making love to the tweeny among the gooseberry bushes; the clothes blown out hard on the line; the dead man in the gutter; the apple tree, stark in the moonlight; the rat swarming with maggots; the lustre dripping blue — our white wax was streaked and stained by each of these differently. Louis was disgusted by the nature of human flesh; Rhoda by our cruelty; Susan could not share; Neville wanted order; Jinny love; and so on. We suffered terribly as we became separate bodies. (Ibid., p. 241)

But after the suffering, healing comes, a wholeness symbolized by the supraordinate personalities Bernard mentions in his final monologue: Hamlet, Shelley, the hero of the Dostoevsky novel, Napoleon, Byron. Not until he ceases identifying with these personalities, however, does the wholeness come: "I, I, I; not Byron, Shelley, Dostoevsky, but I, Bernard." Realizing the Self, he repeats his name and buys

> a picture of Beethoven in a silver frame. Not that I love music, but because the whole of life, its masters, its adven-

turers then appeared in long ranks of magnificent human beings behind me; and I was the inheritor; I, the continuer; I, the person miraculously appointed to carry it on. (Ibid., pp. 253–254)

I disagree with Lyndall Gordon's statement that "the six people in *The Waves* do not change" (1984, p. 221), for clearly they do change. Psychically, they gradually become a whole in Bernard. Gordon is more to the point when she comments about the six speaking characters as they gather to bid Percival goodbye: "Together, the six compose one summation of the species, body, mind, and soul" (ibid., p. 220). As in *Tristram of Lyonesse*, it is love that brings them together — in this case love for Percival (Woolf 1931, p. 125). Susan is domestic, a mother, "wholly woman, purely feminine" (ibid., p. 248). Jinny has many lovers, among them Bernard. She is "honest, an animal" (ibid., p. 266), and she represents an early stage of the anima, the physical, sexual stage. Rhoda, in Gordon's words, has "imaginative fertility" (1984, p. 221) and is the character "who most resembles Virginia Woolf" (ibid., p. 222). She is "obsessed with mortality" (ibid., p. 232), yet she represents, as we shall see, a higher, spiritual level of the anima for Bernard. Neville is intellectual (a Latin scholar like A. E. Housman) and homosexual; his love for Percival is physical as well as spiritual. He enjoys the "hazards of intimacy" (ibid., p. 226), and as a gay man he symbolizes something in all men — the possibility of homosexual love. At his commerical office, Louis is the practical male. He has a relationship with Rhoda and, like her, feels himself an outsider. Yet he, too, is part of the whole, part of the "red carnation," as Bernard says, "that stood in the vase on the table of the restaurant when we dined together with Percival, [and] is become a six-sided flower; made of six lives" (Woolf 1931, p. 229). Together, they've made "One life," for every person has the potential of all the others: the feminine (the mother and the sexually active woman), the masculine (heterosexual and homosexual), the outsider, the intellectual, and the physically active, the hero — Percival.

Bernard has, throughout the novel, developed all four functions of consciousness. Early on he develops a typically masculine function, sensation: "hot towels," he says, "envelop me, and their roughness, as I rub my back, makes my blood purr. Rich and heavy sensations form on the roof of my mind" (ibid., p. 26). A writer, like Orlando, he constantly searches for phrases, exercising his thinking function, "the double capacity to feel, to reason" (ibid., p. 77). Exercising the feeling function, he says "life is pleasant, life is tolerable" (ibid., p. 257). After Percival's death, Bernard begins to use the typically feminine intuitive function. In a gallery, the pictures "expand my [Bernard's] consciousness of him [Percival] and bring him back to me differently. I remember his beauty." And Bernard is nearly persuaded that he "too can be heroic" (ibid., p. 156). He declares in his final monologue: "I was like one admitted behind the scenes: like one shown how the effects are produced" (ibid., p. 266). He intuits that "it is the effort and the struggle, it is the perpetual warfare, it is the shattering and piecing together — this is the daily battle, defeat or victory, the absorbing pursuit" (ibid., pp. 269–270).

The object of their thought and love, the one embedded deep in their collective psyche, is Percival, the natural leader. Bernard sees him in India regarded by the people there as "what indeed he is — a God" (ibid., p. 136). "Look now, how everybody follows Percival," says Louis. "His magnificence is that of some mediaeval commander" (ibid., p. 37). In Arthurian legend, Percival, Galahad, and Bors are the only knights who get to view the Holy Grail. Emma Jung and Marie-Louise von Franz recognize the medieval Percival's "role as a Christ-like redeemer figure" (1980, p. 77). "He forms," they write, "a parallel figure to the *homo altus* or *homo quadratus* of alchemy, the true and total man or the divine component in man which gradually emerges from the depths of the maternal womb of the unconscious and releases specific areas of the psyche previously cut off from life" (ibid., p. 110). Like the Percival of legend, Bernard's friend becomes in death a supraordinate personality, not unlike the figure E. Jung and von Franz describe, a figure who can unite into wholeness unconscious components previously "cut off" from consciousness. This twentieth-century Percival symbolizes a way to the modern day grail of the Self.

Thrown from his horse in India, the Percival of *The Waves* has struggled and died, living an outward, conscious existence, becoming in death a healing archetypal symbol. Bernard's ultimate struggle is internal. He has to battle and accommodate the shadow within: "the old brute . . . the savage, the hairy man who dabbles his fingers in ropes of entrails . . . I have great difficulty sometimes in controlling him." But doing so has its benefits: "He has led me wild dances!" (Woolf 1931, pp. 289–290).

And all of the other characters' assets and defects, from Neville's homosexuality and intellectual capacity to Rhoda's fear of the physical and her suicide to Susan's identification with nature ("I think I am the field . . . I am the trees" (ibid., p. 97)), traits of both sexes, positive and negative, Bernard absorbs, so that he says, "I do not always know if I am man or woman, Bernard or Neville, ·Louis, Susan, Jinny or Rhoda" (ibid., p. 281).

Psychically, the men — Louis and Neville — symbolize the shadow which Bernard has incorporated into his consciousness. The women — Jinny, Susan, and Rhoda — are aspects of the anima. Jinny is a physical, romantic stage. "I can image nothing beyond the circle cast by my body," she says (ibid., pp. 128–129). Susan is the nurturing mother. Her urge is toward life. Like Jinny, she's chthonic, connected with the earth, a connection particularly natural for a woman. Rhoda, chthonic in her obsession with mortality, represents the other side of the anima, the urge toward reabsorption in the primal unity. She has difficulty connecting with "the whole and indivisible mass that you call life" (ibid., p. 130). She seems at times to be play-acting at life. She leaves Louis because she "feared embraces." "My path," she says,

> has been up and up, towards some solitary tree with a pool
> beside it on the very top . . . Who then comes with me?
> Flowers only, the cowbind and the moonlight coloured may.
> . . . Rippling small, rippling grey, innumerable waves spread
> beneath us. . . . We may sink and settle on the waves. The
> sea will drum in my ears. Rolling me over the waves will
> shoulder me under. Everything falls in a tremendous
> shower, dissolving me. (Ibid., pp. 205–206)

We have the same sense here as we had in Swinburne's *Tristram of Lyonesse* of death in the sea as a positive return to primal unity. Yet somehow as an individual Rhoda never seems fully integrated. As a symbol of the anima with her instinctual acceptance of death (a spiritual awareness), she contributes to Bernard's individuation.

In the center, always, is Percival, symbolizing the wholeness of the Self, a transcendent symbol combining the masculine number of wholeness — four, of which he is a part — with the feminine number of wholeness — three — to make the complete seven, a number which, as Cirlot comments, symbolizes "perfect order, a complete period or cycle. It comprises the union of the ternary and the quaternary, and hence it is endowed with exceptional value" (1962, p. 223).

As he approaches death, "an elderly man" (Woolf 1931, p. 285), Bernard contemplates, in fact takes on,

> the mystery of things . . . I can visit the remote verges of the
> desert lands where the savage sits by the campfire. Day rises;
> the girl lifts the watery fire-hearted jewels to her brow; the
> sun levels his beams straight at the sleeping house; the waves
> deepen their bars; they fling themselves on shore; back blows

the spray; sweeping their waters they surround the boat and the sea-holly. (Ibid., pp. 291–292)

Poetically, he remarks: "The birds sing in chorus; deep tunnels run between the stalks of flowers; the house is whitened; the sleeper stretches; gradually all is astir" (ibid., p. 292). And he realizes that instead of "a temple, a church, a whole universe," he's merely "what you see—an elderly man, rather heavy, grey above the ears" (ibid.). In other words, he has the ability to see himself as he is and to accept himself thus. He is becoming an integrated personality: "there is a gradual coming together, running into one, acceleration and unification." As he leaves the restaurant where he has dined with a person he thinks he met on a "ship going to Africa" (ibid., p. 238), he regains "the sense of the complexity and the reality and the struggle" (ibid., p. 294). He senses "some sort of renewal" as the dawn arrives, the eternal cycle of life—"the incessant rise and fall and fall and rise again." He has a moment of self-revelation, what Virginia Woolf might call a "moment of being":

> And in me too the wave rises. It swells; it arches its back. I am aware once more of a new desire, something rising beneath me like the proud horse whose rider first spurs and then pulls him back. What enemy do we now perceive advancing against us, you whom I ride now, as we stand pawing this stretch of pavement? It is death. Death is the enemy. It is against whom I ride with my spear couched and my hair flying back like a young man's, like Percival's, when he galloped in India. I strike spurs into my horse. Against you I will fling myself, unvanquished and unyielding, O Death! (Ibid., p. 297)

Why is death still the enemy? It is because Bernard is not ready yet for a final realization of the Self. *"The waves broke on the shore."* There the novel ends, with an elderly Bernard integrated, fully androgynous, affirming life, ready to press on toward a later, final individuation, thinking of Percival, a symbol of the Self.

Notes

1. Bazin implies this, but doesn't say it. I should point out, in addition, that hers is not a Jungian study as such. Maud Bodkin, in her monumental study, *Archetypal Patterns in Poetry: Psychological Studies of Imagination*, does touch on some of the archetypal aspects of *Orlando*, but her approach is not specifically Jungian (1934, pp. 300–307).

2. It is interesting to note that Vita Sackville-West, about and for whom *Orlando* was written, in writing about the genesis of that book maintains that Virginia Woolf "was at heart a born romantic" (1955, p. 157).

3. Actually, Jung is redundant here. All complexes, he decided, are autonomous. That is, the person who has the complex cannot consciously control it. In *Modern Man in Search of a Soul*, he writes that

   > complexes are psychic contents which are outside the control of the conscious mind. They have been split off from consciousness and lead a separate existence in the unconscious, being at all times ready to hinder or to reinforce the conscious intentions. (1933, p. 79)

   Complexes, like archetypes, from which they derive (See Samuels, Shorter, and Plaut 1986, p. 34), can be positive or negative, and they do "not necessarily indicate inferiority" (Jung 1933, p. 79). They can function as stimuli to further development, or they can be obstacles to the same. As such, they are "focal or nodal points of psychic life which we would not wish to do without. Indeed they must not be lacking, for otherwise psychic activity would come to a fatal standstill" (Jung 1933, p. 79).

4. I am grateful to Nigel Nicolson and Joanne Trautmann, who let me see the proof of this third volume of the *Letters* at Sissinghurst Castle, Kent, on July 9, 1977, before the volume was published (I was working on an earlier version of this chapter that first appeared in *Modern Fiction Studies* (1979)). Parts of these letters had been published by Sackville-West in *The Listener*, January 27, 1955, and by Quentin Bell, in *Virginia Woolf: A Biography*. Sackville-West changes details that pertain to her private life. For example, in the October 13–14, letter, Sackville-West has Woolf writing: "Tomorrow I begin the chapter which describes you and Sasha meeting on the ice." In fact, Woolf had written "Violet" instead of "Sasha." Of course, the character of Sasha is based on Violet Trefusis, with whom Vita had had a long and tumultuous romantic affair (see Nicolson 1973).

5. I do not mean to imply that those of Woolf's novels written prior to *Orlando* are entirely without humor. She has flashes of humor that are not often acknowledged. The *tone* of *Orlando*, however, is far more lighthearted than any of the previous books. The only other book with a similar tone is *Flush: A Biography* (1933), a far less substantial work. And *A Room of One's Own* (1929) contains plenty of satirical humor.

6. Bodkin does not use the Jungian terms. I use them because I think they shed psychological light on the meaning of the symbols. On the stages of the anima and the animus, see von Franz (1964, pp. 184–185, 194–195).

7. Eileen B. Sypher writes that Bernard "suggests himself as a representation of the androgynous artist Woolf speaks of in *A Room of One's Own*" (1983, p. 187). But Sypher argues with Woolf's ideas about androgyny: "Conceptually, androgyny, while promising union, perpetuates division as it tends to suggest there are identifiable, essential 'male' and 'female' perceptions and behavior. . . . Politically the concept is also troublesome, as the debates in feminist criticism on this issue have observed" (ibid., p. 189). Sypher finds that "One of the most disturbing things about *The Waves* is that Woolf houses a self-consciously androgynous spirit in a male body, not even attempting to alter genitalia as she does in *Orlando*" (ibid., p. 191). Sypher raises questions that cannot be thoroughly explored here. It seems to me she is begging the issue in her objection to "a self-consciously androgynous spirit in a male body" in *The Waves*; Orlando, after all, *is* a woman, although she begins as a man. Jung has been criticized for delineating specific male and female traits or principles, yet, as Jungian analyst Anthony Stevens writes: "there is no question of one [masculine or feminine principle] being 'superior' to the other; both are mutually complementary, homeostatically balanced and mutually interdependent." Jung, Stevens says, "argued that *both* [masculine and feminine principles] were at work in every human individual, regardless of his or her biologically assigned sexual identity" (1982, p. 175). Furthermore, Stevens offers recent biological evidence for psychological differences between the sexes (ibid., pp. 180–203). Laurens van der Post has said Jung "had an instinct that what was wrong with life, what made life tear apart, made it incomplete" was that "the feminine was rejected, driven insane, driven mad by a world of men, rejected by a masculine-dominated world" (interview in Wagner 1983). Perhaps this instinct Jung had and his emphasis on the equality of anima/animus is what drew so many women to him who became Jungian analysts. (Barbara Hannah, Marie-Louise von Franz, and Jolande Jacobi are but three of many examples.) For those interested in a thorough examination of the topic of androgyny by a well-known Jungian analyst, I suggest June Singer's *Androgyny: The Opposites Within*. "Androgyny," writes Singer, "is innate in each individual" (1989, p. 203).

8. Royalties from the sale of Virginia Woolf's books were sufficient to support the extensive work required to prepare her diary for publication (Bell 1977–1984, vol. 5, p. xiv). This fact plus the continued interest in and sales of her letters, diary, and other writings are further indications of the popularity of Virginia Woolf's work.

9. Leonard Woolf notes that his wife "wanted to show that these six persons [in *The Waves*] were severally facets of a single complete person" (quoted by Warner 1987, p. 74). Bazin writes of these characters: "It is a sense of oneness . . . not solitude, which actually eliminates the characters' consciousness of their separate identities" (1973, p. 149). And Linda Kathryn Overstreet feels "Bernard represents the psychological culmination of mankind. . . . After mid-

dle age, Bernard experiences Jung's process of individuation, in which he assumes the archetypal nature of each of the other characters thus joining them symbolically as a psychologically whole being." Overstreet also analyzes "the recurrent image [of the mandala] throughout *The Waves*" (1982, p. 3316A), an image introduced by Bernard as the very first speaker in the novel: " 'I see a ring,' said Bernard, 'hanging above me. It quivers and hangs in a loop of light' " (Woolf 1931, p. 9). Overstreet also has an interesting and valid interpretation of the three woman characters as "three aspects of the Great Mother archetype." However, she also says: "Neville demonstrates negative powers of the Great Mother in his homosexuality, in his inability to reconcile life with death, and in his wish to be rejoined with the mother" (Overstreet 1982, p. 3316A). Rhoda has a similar wish, yet ultimately it is no more negative — in Woolf's treatment — than Neville's. Neville's homosexuality, as I indicate below, represents a potential aspect, neither positive nor negative, in the sexuality of every person. For Neville, it is a positive trait, for it is natural to him; it represents part of his personal myth.

Works Cited

Bazin, Nancy Topping. 1973. *Virginia Woolf and the Androgynous Vision.* New Brunswick, N.J.: Rutgers University Press.

Bell, Anne Olivier, ed. 1977–1984. *The Diary of Virginia Woolf.* 5 vols. New York: Harcourt.

Bodkin, Maud. 1934. *Archetypal Patterns in Poetry: Psychological Studies of Imagination.* London: Oxford University Press.

Cirlot, J. E. 1962. *A Dictionary of Symbols.* Jack Sage, trans. New York: Philosophical Library.

Gordon, Lyndall. 1984. *Virginia Woolf: A Writer's Life.* New York: Norton.

Gorsky, Susan Rubinow. 1978. *Virginia Woolf.* Boston: Twayne.

Jacobi, Jolande. 1968. *The Psychology of C. G. Jung: An Introduction with Illustrations.* Ralph Manheim, trans. New Haven, Conn.: Yale University Press.

Jung, C. G. 1921. *Psychological Types. CW*, vol. 6. Princeton, N.J.: Princeton University Press, 1971.

_____. 1931. On the relation of analytical psychology to poetry. *CW* 15:65–83. Princeton, N.J.: Princeton University Press, 1966.

_____. 1933. *Modern Man in Search of a Soul.* W. S. Dell and Cary F. Baynes, trans. New York: Harcourt.

_____. 1950. Psychology and literature. *CW* 15:84–107. Princeton, N.J.: Princeton University Press, 1966.

_____. 1963. *Memories, Dreams, Reflections*. Richard and Clara Winston, trans. Aniela Jaffé, ed. New York: Vintage.

Jung, Emma, and von Franz, Marie-Louise. 1980. *The Grail Legend*. Andrea Dykes, trans. 2nd ed. Boston: Sigo.

Majumbar, Robin, and McLaurin, Allen. 1975. *Virginia Woolf: The Critical Heritage*. London: Routledge.

Nicolson, Nigel, and Trautmann, Joanne, eds. 1975–1980. *The Letters of Virginia Woolf*. 6 vols. New York: Harcourt.

Nicolson, Nigel. 1973. *Portrait of a Marriage*. New York: Atheneum.

Overstreet, Linda Kathryn. 1982. "This Globe, Full of Figures": an archetypal study of Virginia Woolf's *The Waves*. *Dissertation Abstracts International* 43: 3316A.

Richter, Harvena. 1970. *Virginia Woolf: The Inward Voyage*. Princeton, N.J.: Princeton University Press.

Rose, Phyllis. 1978. *Woman of Letters: A Life of Virginia Woolf*. San Diego: Harcourt.

Sackville-West, V. 1947. *Knole and the Sackvilles*. London: Lindsay Drummond.

_____. 1955. Virginia Woolf and "Orlando." *The Listener*, January 27, 1955, pp. 157–158.

Samuels, Andrew, Shorter, Bani, and Plaut, Fred. 1986. *A Critical Dictionary of Jungian Analysis*. London: Routledge.

Singer, June. 1989. *Androgyny: The Opposites Within*. 2nd ed. Boston: Sigo.

Snider, Clifton. 1977. C. G. Jung's analytical psychology and literary criticism. *Psychocultural Review* 1:96–108, 216–242.

Stevens, Anthony. 1982. *Archetypes: A Natural History of the Self*. New York: Quill.

Sypher, Eileen B. 1983. *The Waves*: A Utopia of Androgyny? In *Virginia Woolf: Centennial Essays*. Elaine K. Ginsberg and Laura Moss Gottlieb, eds. Troy, N.Y.: Whitston.

Trautmann, Joanne. 1973. *The Jessamy Brides: The Friendship of Virginia Woolf and V. Sackville-West*. University Park, Penn.: Pennsylvania State University Press.

Wagner, S. 1983. *Matter of Heart*. M. Whitney, dir. M. Whitney, prod. Los Angeles: C. G. Jung Institute, Kino International Corp., 1987. Videocassette.

Warner, Eric. 1987. *Virginia Woolf*: The Waves. Cambridge: Cambridge University Press.

Woolf, Leonard. 1960–1969. *Downhill All the Way: An Autobiography of the*

Years 1919 to 1939. Vol. 4 of *The Autobiography of Leonard Woolf*. New York: Harcourt, 1967.

Woolf, Virginia. 1928. *Orlando: A Biography*. New York: Harcourt, 1956.

_____. 1929. *A Room of One's Own*. New York: Harcourt.

_____. 1931. *The Waves*. San Diego: Harcourt, 1959.

von Franz, Marie-Louise. 1964. The process of individuation. In *Man and His Symbols*. C. G. Jung, ed. Garden City, N.Y.: Doubleday.

Chapter Six

Two Myths for Our Time:
Carson McCullers's
The Member of the Wedding and
*Clock Without Hands**

*Yes, the earth had revolved its seasons and spring
had come again. But there was no longer a revulsion
against nature, against things. A strange lightness
had come upon his soul and he exalted. He looked at nature
now and it was part of himself. He was no longer a man
watching a clock without hands.*

Carson McCullers,
Clock Without Hands

In her comparatively brief life, Carson McCullers produced fiction that still has relevance for us in the last years of the twentieth century. *The Member of the Wedding* (1946) is probably her most popular work, and some critics feel it is her finest. Lawrence Graver, for example, writes: "Because the things that go on in *The Member of the Wedding* are available to everyone and are recorded with vivacity by an artist who understands them, it is the best of all her books" (1969, p. 33). Written during World War II, when the world was collectively split, *The Member of the Wedding* is an unconscious attempt — an attempt, indeed, from the collective unconscious — to compensate for that split. Just as the world badly needed wholeness, so does Frankie Addams, the lonely imaginative twelve-year-old protagonist of the novel and the play (which opened on Broadway on January 5, 1950). McCullers's last novel, *Clock Without Hands* (1961), a best-seller when it was first published (Carr 1975, p. 494), speaks especially to our age, for it deals with, among other relevant themes, the theme of death and dying from terminal illness. In these two novels, McCullers created myths for our time, and a Jungian examination of these novels will demonstrate new levels of meaning in them and elicit, I hope, a greater appreciation of McCullers's art.

I

The genesis of *The Member of the Wedding* illustrates nicely Jung's theory of creativity. In fact, McCullers's beliefs about creativity are similar to those of Jung. In reference to the creative process, she writes: "After months of confusion and labor, when the idea has flowered, the collusion is Divine. It always comes from the subconscious and cannot be controlled" (1971, p. 275). She goes on to give an example of such a collusion: when she was writing *The Heart Is a Lonely Hunter* (1940), she hit upon the idea that her main character, Harry Minowitz, was a deaf mute. Instantly she changed his name to John Singer. McCullers's biographers have shown how a similar inspiration seized McCullers when she was writing *The Member of the Wedding*. She had been working on the novel for some time without finding a clear direction for it. Then, on Thanksgiving Day, 1940, she and the other members of the artistic ménage at 7 Middagh Street, Brooklyn Heights, were having coffee and brandy when they heard the sound of a fire engine siren.[1] McCullers and Gypsy Rose Lee went out to follow it. After running a few blocks, McCullers received her spark of illumination. Grabbing Lee by the arm, McCullers burst out: "Frankie is in love with her brother and his bride, and wants to become a member of the wedding." Later McCullers said that "Gypsy . . . stared at me as though I had lost my mind" (Evans 1965, p. 98).[2]

In writing *The Member of the Wedding*, McCullers created archetypal images to compensate for contemporary imbalance. In other words, she made a myth for our time; today, as in the forties, humanity is in need of wholeness and growth, just as Frankie is in need of psychic wholeness and growth. The plot is very simple. Her mother being dead, Frankie lives alone in a large house with her father, but she spends most of her waking hours in the kitchen with her six-year-old cousin, John Henry West, and the middle-aged black cook, Berenice Sadie Brown, "a stout, motherly Negro woman with an air of great capability and devoted protection."[3] As John B. Vickery points out, they "represent the worlds of the child and adult which Frankie is endeavoring to fuse" (1960, p. 22). However, as I will show, they are more than childhood and adulthood: they are personifications in the dreamlike world McCullers has created of the archetypal Child, Mother, and Wise Old Woman. Frankie has an older brother, a soldier named Jarvis, who comes home from Alaska with Janice, a young woman from a town farther north, Winter Hill. Jarvis announces his plans to marry Janice. Frankie, who is sick of her environment, is struck by the idea that she will join Jarvis and Janice in the wedding and thereafter depart with them for unknown and exciting regions. The idea transforms her life, and she becomes obsessed by it, ignoring the advice of Berenice.

Both her name and her appearance ("her hair had been cut like a boy's") indicate her androgynous personality, but this fusion of opposites is on the surface only: she is not whole psychologically. Her last name also suggests her case is primal; she is an "everyperson." Jung believes that every person has a personal myth (van der Post 1975, p. 118), and Frankie's myth is that she and her brother Jarvis and his bride Janice are to be united:

> *They are the we of me.* Yesterday, and all the twelve years of her life, she had only been Frankie. She was an *I* person who had to walk around and do things by herself. All other people had a *we* to claim, all other except her. When Berenice said *we*, she meant Honey and Big Mama, her lodge, or her church. The *we* of her father was the store. All members of clubs have a *we* to belong to and talk about. The soldiers in the army can say *we*, and even the criminals on chain-gangs. But the old Frankie had had no *we* to claim, unless it would be the terrible summer *we* of her and John Henry and Berenice — and that was the last *we* in the world she wanted. Now all this was suddenly over with and changed. There was her brother and the bride, and it was as though when first she saw them something she had known inside of her: *They are the we of me.* (McCullers 1951, p. 646)

Just as the soldiers of the United States had traveled to war around the world, so Frankie in her adolescent fantasy planned to travel with her brother and sister-in-law after the wedding.

Frankie has become possessed by the archetype of the quest and the Eden myth. In traveling with Jarvis and Janice, Frankie would be escaping her environment: the hot summer, which "was like a green sick dream, or like a silent crazy jungle under glass," the "black and shrunken" town, her "old ugly house," and the "sad and ugly" kitchen where she spends most of her time with John Henry and Berenice. First, the wedding would take place in Winter Hill, a hundred miles to the north. Frankie associates Winter Hill with Alaska, where her soldier brother had been stationed. She connects Winter Hill "with dreams of Alaska and cold snow" (ibid., p.

604). Second, Frankie imagines "bright flowered islands . . . China, Peachville, New Zealand, Paris, Cincinnati, Rome. . . . But still she did not know where she should go" (ibid., p. 640).

Although she doesn't know where she will go, her fervent wish is to go, as it were, to an Eden of her imagination. That her world is governed by the unconscious is indicated by the many references throughout the novel to dreams and craziness — both expressions of the archetypes, as is fantasy, in which she freely indulges.[4] The desire to journey from the dull but real world of her own town to unknown Edens is in fact an evasion of the task before her: to achieve inner growth and maturity. As Laurens van der Post shows, Jung came to believe that often travel "for sheer travel's sake" was a "substitute, *Ersatz* journey for a far more difficult and urgent journey modern man was called upon to undertake into the unknown universe of himself" (1975, p. 51).

Frankie has also become possessed by the archetype of the *hieros gamos*, or the "sacred wedding," an archetype of wholeness, symbolizing the union of opposites. Thinking about the wedding, Frankie sees "a silent church, a strange snow slanting down against the colored windows" (McCullers 1951, p. 600). Jung writes: "When a situation occurs which corresponds to a given archetype, that archetype becomes activated and a compulsiveness appears, which, like an instinctual drive, gains its way against all reason and will"(1936–1937, p. 48).[5] These words describe Frankie's situation exactly. After seeing her brother and his bride, after coming to the compulsive realization that she was "going off with the two of them to whatever place that they will go," Frankie is convinced she knows who she is, and her goal is undivided: she will be a member of the wedding; she will go with the married couple (McCullers 1951, p. 650). No longer do the old questions, "who she was and what she would be in the world," bother her (ibid., p. 651). She is no longer unconnected. She is going someplace, and never mind what reason — available to her in the words of Berenice — says to the contrary.

While John Henry symbolizes the archetypal Child, Berenice, the middle-aged black cook with the blue glass eye, symbolizes two archetypes: the Mother and the Wise Old Woman. Frankie's biological mother had died just after Frankie was born. Berenice, as one scholar has put it, "is as responsive to Frankie as a mother would be" (Wikborg 1975, p. 7). Berenice fits into the archetypal motif of the dual mother, wherein the hero is raised by a foster mother (Oedipus and Moses are examples). "The dual-mother motif," writes Jung, "suggests the idea of a dual birth. One of the mothers is the real, human mother, the other is the symbolical mother

. . . she is distinguished as being divine, supernatural, or in some way extraordinary" (1926, p. 322). While Frankie is hardly a hero of the stature of Oedipus or Moses, she is symbolic of the individual, the "everyperson," in the twentieth century and his or her needs. Indeed, she is an antihero like Holden Caulfield, an older version of herself.

My calling Berenice an example of the dual mother motif may appear farfetched because she does not seem "divine, supernatural, or in some way extraordinary," but actually she is numinous in a way uncommon to most women in her position. Like Tiresias, the blind prophet of Thebes, the one-eyed Berenice has, in the words of Baldanza, "spiritual vision . . . the more intense for her physical handicap" (1958, p. 158). When she recites the history of her marriages, she makes "each sentence like a song . . . in a chanting kind of voice" (McCullers 1951, p. 708). The recitation is a kind of primitive ritual, and, when Frankie becomes possessed by the archetype of the wedding, she is for the first time able to believe in love and be "included in the conversation as a person who understood and had worth-while opinions" (Ibid., p. 716).

Frankie needs the advice of her symbolic Mother because she is going through a rite of initiation, an indication of which is the fact she has in her mind changed her name to F. Jasmine. Initiates traditionally take on new names. Additionally, both Frankie and Berenice share similar "visions" in seeing their love-objects (Jarvis and Janice and Ludie Freeman, respectively) out of the corners of their eyes when the love-objects are not actually present. To confirm Frankie's new status, Berenice allows Frankie to smoke one of her hand-rolled cigarettes as one of "two grown people smoking at the dinner table" (ibid., p. 717).

Throughout the novel Berenice is both the symbolic Mother and the Wise Old Woman to Frankie. She gives both Frankie and John Henry the love and nourishment of a mother, but to Frankie she gives more—her advice and experience as a woman. To Berenice, Frankie's obsession with the wedding is a "mania" that is "pure foolishness" (ibid., p. 692). Her advice frequently comes in the form of "known sayings," folk wisdom such as "Two is company and three is a crowd. And that is the main thing about a wedding" (ibid., p. 690). However, it is Berenice's experience that is potentially of most benefit to Frankie, although Frankie chooses to pursue her obsession with the wedding despite Berenice's warning. Most people who are possessed by archetypes do choose to pursue their obsessions.

Berenice herself is possessed by an archetype, that of Ideal Love.[6] Of all her four husbands, Berenice's first, Ludie Freeman, was the only one she truly loved, and when they were together, she tells Frankie:

> "There was no human woman in all the world more happy
> than I was in them days. . . . And that includes everybody.
> . . . It includes all queens and millionaires and first ladies of
> the land. And I mean it includes people of all color. You hear
> me, Frankie? No human woman in all the world was hap-
> pier than Berenice Sadie Brown." (Ibid., p. 718)

Berenice's mistake was that after Ludie died she tried to find another man
to fill his role as the ideal mate. Searching for another Ludie, she married
her second husband because his thumb resembled Ludie's; she married her
third because his build resembled Ludie's and he had bought Ludie's coat,
which Berenice had had to sell to pay for a proper funeral for Ludie.
Berenice's fourth husband was the worst, "so terrible that Berenice had
had to call the Law on him" (ibid., p. 728).

In telling Frankie about her past, Berenice has a purpose — to warn
Frankie about the danger of her obsession with the wedding, "the saddest
piece of foolishness I ever knew" (ibid., p. 725). Although Frankie is
rapidly growing away from her child ego state, she is unable to heed
Berenice's warning. Frankie has to act out her obsession with the archetypes in order to learn the lesson Berenice has been trying to teach her. The
Wise Old Woman has traveled a similar road, but the hero — or antihero —
must travel her own road; she must fulfill her own destiny. Berenice, at
least, is able to learn the lesson she is trying to teach, for at the end of the
novel she has given up her search for Ideal Love and has instead decided to
marry T. T. Williams (ibid., p. 785), "a fine upstanding colored gentleman," who "has walked in a state of grace all of his life," but who, nevertheless, doesn't make her "shiver," as Ludie had (ibid., p. 709). She has
opted for the real as opposed to the ideal.

By choosing reality as opposed to fantasy, Berenice is instructing
Frankie through her actions as well as her words, despite the fact that by
the time Berenice has chosen to marry a fifth time she has virtually ceased
to be an influence in Frankie's life. Prior to this time, however, Berenice
has always been an example of a mature woman, a kind of role model for
Frankie. Sitting at the kitchen table listening to Berenice, Frankie

> thought of a fact that all her life had seemed to her most
> curious: Berenice always spoke of herself as though she was
> somebody very beautiful. Almost on this one subject,
> Berenice was really not in her right mind. F. Jasmine lis-
> tened to the voice and stared at Berenice across the table: the
> dark face with the wild blue eye, the eleven greased plaits

that fitted her head like a skull-cap, the wide flat nose that quivered as she spoke. And whatever else Berenice might be, she was not beautiful. (Ibid., pp. 697–698)

What Frankie does not understand is that despite Berenice's appearance (and in spite of her illusions about finding another Ludie), Berenice is mature enough to have developed a positive self-image.

Margaret B. McDowell has suggested an explanation for Berenice's choice of a blue artificial eye. Berenice "perhaps attempts to achieve in this choice a linking of the worlds of the Negro and the white" (McDowell 1980, p. 81). McCullers may very well have intended such an implication, but on the level of the collective unconscious the joining of black and white (the functioning brown eye with the glass blue eye) shows an urge toward psychic wholeness for Berenice and for Frankie. Indeed, Frankie projects her own need for wholeness onto Berenice. After reflecting in the passage quoted above that Berenice "was not beautiful," Frankie decides to give Berenice some advice: "I think you ought to quit worrying about beaus and be content with T. T." (McCullers 1951, p. 698). The Wise Old Woman in this particular instance is not so wise she could not learn from her adolescent antihero.

Jung's analytical psychology primarily concerns itself with the second half of life, the stage of the individuation process in which the individual's task is to accommodate the contrasexual, the anima in man, the animus in woman. *The Member of the Wedding*, however, is concerned with the first half of life, with adolescent psychology. The first half of life, "through consolidation of the ego, differentiation of the main function and of the dominant attitude type, and development of an appropriate persona . . . aims at the adaptation of the individual to the demands of his environment" (Jacobi 1968, p. 108). These are the issues with which Frankie should be concerned.

Frankie has yet to consolidate her ego: it is clearly unstable. Her "attitude type" is extraversion, for her libido (that is, her psychic energy) flows outward, but she has not differentiated her main function. I refer to Jung's functions of consciousness: thinking, feeling, sensation, and intuition. Frankie has developed a little of each of these: she asks fundamental questions about her life, thus using the thinking function; she makes judgments as to right and wrong (as in her conception of the ideal world (McCullers 1951, pp. 713–714)), thus using the feeling function; she relates to the world through her senses (her knife throwing is an example), thus using the sensation function; and she shares with Berenice an ability to recognize "signs" and, as in her fears for Honey, potential danger, thus using the intuition function.

But none of these functions has she developed as her main function. She is trying them out; her personality is still forming. When she has developed a main function, she will need to integrate the other functions into her consciousness as fully as possible. Last, Frankie is far from developing "an appropriate persona." The persona is the "mask" or conscious public identity an individual assumes. Frances, the name Frankie prefers after the shattering experience of the wedding, cannot decide whether she will be "a great poet — or else the foremost authority on radar" (Ibid., p. 787).

Although Frankie has masculine aspects in her personality (she is the "best knife-thrower in this town" (ibid., p. 639) and the knife is an obvious masculine symbol), she has yet to accommodate the masculine — symbolized by the animus — in her psyche. That task will come in later life. To grow up, she has to break with her father and her foster mother. The previous April her father, with whom she had been sleeping, decides she is now "too big" to sleep with him, and "she began to have a grudge against her father" (ibid., p. 625). The break with her father was necessary, and now she is ready for a symbolic rebirth from the womblike kitchen. That the kitchen is symbolic of the womb — and hence the unconscious — is suggested by "the queer drawings of Christmas trees, airplanes, freak soldiers, flowers" on its walls (ibid., p. 606). These childish drawings, drawn by John Henry and Frankie herself, give the room "a crazy look, like that of a room in the crazy-house" (ibid., p. 602). It was his experience at a "crazy-house," the Burghölzli mental Hospital in Zürich, that gave Jung some of his first evidence of the collective unconscious and the archetypes (1963, p. 127). As the summer wears on, the drawings begin to "bother" Frankie: "The kitchen looked strange to her, and she was afraid" (McCullers 1951, p. 606). To paraphrase Saint Paul, she is ready to put away childish things.

Lonely and afraid, she is not fully aware of this. Without any adolescent friends, she clings to her six-year-old cousin, John Henry, inviting him to spend the night, as she has done frequently since she has been unable to sleep with her father. "I thought you were sick and tired of him," says Berenice upon being told Frankie has invited John Henry again to spend the night.

> "I am sick and tired of him," said Frankie. "But it seemed to me he looked scared."
> "Scared of what?"

Frankie shook her head. "Maybe I mean lonesome," she said finally. (Ibid., p. 606)

Frankie is, of course, projecting — attributing to John Henry her own problems. The following day she again asks John Henry to spend the night. This time he is reluctant, and Frankie responds by screaming: "Fool jackass! . . . I only asked you because I thought you look so ugly and so lonesome" (ibid., p. 647).

Frankie's problem is at root a spiritual one; indeed, McCullers herself has written: "I suppose my central theme is the theme of spiritual isolation" (1958, p. viii). Here the role of John Henry as the archetype of the Child becomes significant. Jung refers to the "numinous character" of the child, and maintains " 'Child' means something evolving towards independence" (Jung and Kerényi 1963, p. 87). In John Henry, Frankie unconsciously sees the child in herself evolving toward independence and, quite naturally, she is afraid. All archetypes, however, have a dual nature, and, paradoxically, the child symbolizes "both beginning and end, [he is] an initial and a terminal creature" (ibid., p. 97). Furthermore, Jung states:

> Psychologically speaking, this means that the 'child' symbolizes the pre-conscious and post-conscious essence of man. His pre-conscious essence is the unconscious state of earliest childhood; his post-conscious essence is an anticipation by analogy of life after death. In this idea the all-embracing nature of psychic wholeness is expressed. (Ibid., p. 97)

When John Henry makes a "perfect little biscuit man" which reminds Frankie of John Henry himself, his symbolic wholeness is suggested (McCullers 1951, p. 607). His consciousness is still in a nascent state, not fully differentiated yet. His death near the end of the novel is not only symbolic of the death of Frankie's childhood (see Evans 1965, p. 124), but also an adumbration of the wholeness possible for Frankie.

Frankie's problem is that she is isolated, afraid, "a member of nothing in the world" (McCullers 1951, p. 599). She fears the older girls, who have excluded her, have been "spreading it all over town that I smell bad" (ibid., p. 610), and she is certain if her present rate of growth continues she will be nine feet tall by the time she is eighteen (ibid., p. 618). She will be a freak, like the ones she has seen each year at the Chattahoochee Exposition — the freaks who try "to connect their eyes with hers, as though to say: we know you. She was afraid of their long Freak eyes" (ibid., p.

619). These freaks (which include the "Wild Nigger," the "Pin Head," and the "Half-Man Half-Woman") are personifications of archetypes. She sees something of herself in them through her own eyes, symbolic of a growing consciousness (see Jung 1950, p. 337). Because she does not understand the symbolism of the freaks, she is afraid. Finally, Frankie has become "a criminal. If the Law knew about her, she could be tried in the courthouse and locked up in the jail" (McCullers 1951, p. 622).[7]

All of her fears are symptoms of a deep psychic unrest, and none of them is unusual for a twelve-year-old. Frankie is ready for a change, and she is ripe for an archetype of wholeness—the *hieros gamos*—when it presents itself to her personified by her brother and his bride. She quickly becomes a victim of psychic inflation, which, in the words of Jungian psychologist Frieda Fordham, is "possession" by an archetype, "indicating that the person so possessed has been, as it were, blown up by something too big for himself, something that is not really personal at all, but collective" (1966, p. 61). Thus Frankie imagines she and the wedding couple will be asked "to speak over the radio some day" (McCullers 1951, p. 710). "Things will happen so fast," she says, "we won't hardly have time to realize them. Captain Jarvis Addams sinks twelve Jap battleships and decorated by the President. Miss F. Jasmine Addams breaks all records. Mrs. Janice Addams elected Miss United Nations in beauty contest. One thing after another happening so fast we don't hardly notice them" (ibid., pp. 737–738). Frankie feels "the power of the wedding; it was as though . . . she ought to order and advise" (ibid., p. 754). Specifically, she feels she should warn Honey, Berenice's foster brother, so she advises him to go to Cuba or Mexico—in other words, to travel, as she plans to do, and thereby avoid looking inward, where the real problem and solution lie. Fordham says the "feeling of godlikeness . . . which comes through inflation is an illusion," and Frankie is to suffer severely for the illusion (1966, p. 61).

An important part of the novel, which McCullers merely alludes to in the play, is Frankie's encounter with the soldier at the Blue Moon Motel. Although she has learned a little about sex, Frankie does not accept what she has learned. The older girls who do not admit her to their club, she tells John Henry, "were talking nasty lies about married people" (McCullers 1951, p. 610). So F. Jasmine, despite her new status as indicated by her name, is not at all prepared psychologically or physically, I suspect, for a "date" with a grown man. Archetypally this means she is not ready for an encounter with the animus, the archetype of the male in the female. This encounter will come in later life, if she reaches that stage of individuation.

For now, she has only begun the process of becoming a whole person psychologically. McCullers subtly shows this in several ways. One of the ways is the unfinished scale of the piano-tuner (ibid., p. 700), which hints Frankie is not to achieve complete wholeness in the novel, although she will achieve growth—a new, more mature psychic level. Another of the subtle indications that wholeness is not to be achieved is also vaguely connected with music. Sitting in the dark kitchen after their last meal together (there is a resemblance to the Last Supper), Berenice, John Henry, and F. Jasmine each spontaneously begins to cry, just as in the past they would automatically begin to sing, a separate song each "until at last the tunes began to merge and they sang a special music that the three of them made up together" (ibid., p. 743). Such music they are not to make again. The wholeness and harmony of the womblike kitchen is to be broken, and the crying is both a lament for the loss of their secure world, whatever its limitations, and an indication that the nature of their experience is spiritual.

Before her encounter with the soldier, Frankie visits Big Mama, an old black fortuneteller who lives with Berenice. Oliver Evans has written that Big Mama's "chief function, apart from supplying a touch of the supernatural and a bit of local colour, is to predict the outcome of Frankie's trip to Winter Hill" (1965, p. 114). Yet Big Mama's function is more than this: she is the seer, another version of the Wise Old Woman, and she is another indication that in *The Member of the Wedding* we are in a dreamlike, primal world—a world of archetypes. Frankie does her best to disbelieve Big Mama's fortune, but her rationalization is destroyed by the events of the wedding day. She has looked outside herself for wholeness instead of inside, and she has been bitterly disappointed.[8]

Having failed to persuade Jarvis and Janice to take her with them, Frankie decides to run away that night by herself. John Henry is again sleeping in her bed, and it is he who, albeit inadvertently, alerts Royal Addams that his daughter has run away. Out on the street by herself, in a last vain attempt to evade personal growth, Frankie finds she does not know how to escape: "If there was only somebody to tell her what to do and where to go and how to get there!" (McCullers 1951, p. 780). She still needs a guide, yet, as her decision not to shoot herself with her father's pistol indicates, she has chosen to continue the struggle which eventually leads to individuation or Selfhood—psychic wholeness. But at this moment she seems caught in the world of the unconscious:

> She was back to the fear of the summertime, the old feelings
> that the world was separate from herself — and the failed
> wedding had quickened the fear to terror. There had been a
> time, only yesterday, when she felt that every person that she
> saw was somehow connected with herself and there was
> between the two of them an instant recognition. (Ibid., p.
> 784)

Back in the Blue Moon Hotel, she feels "queer as a person drowning" (ibid., p. 785), and then her father arrives to take her home.

The image of someone drowning is appropriate, for she might well have been permanently and pathologically possessed by the archetype. Luckily, although Frankie has not achieved wholeness, she has been reborn into a more mature psychic state. As the death of the child John Henry symbolizes, Frankie has grown. She is leaving the womb of the summer kitchen and breaking away from Berenice, her symbolic mother, who has served her purpose. This breaking away is a necessary transition for the adolescent. Frankie has yet to come to terms with the masculine in her psyche, symbolized by her father, but she has begun to accommodate the shadow, that other unrecognized part of the psyche personified by a member of the same sex. Her earlier, "criminal" career had been an expression of her shadow, which is now symbolized by her new friend, the Catholic Mary Littlejohn who, unlike Frankie, has lived abroad. Frankie still indulges in fantasy, planning to travel around the world with Mary (ibid., p. 790), but she is "mad about Michelangelo" (ibid., p. 786), who as a supraordinate personality is symbolic of the Self and therefore foreshadows a new awareness for Frankie.

Laurens van der Post, in his biography of Jung, discusses one of Jung's patients at the Burghölzli Mental Hospital. When the patient was healed, she refused anymore to tell Jung her dreams. Van der Post quotes Jung's reaction: "I cannot tell you how moved I was . . . I could have wept for joy because you see at last the dream, the story, was her own again. And at once I discharged her" (1975, p. 126). This anecdote parallels the story of Frankie Addams. After her catastrophic disappointment at the wedding, she never spoke about it again, for the initiate does not reveal what has happened in her rite of passage. The story is "her own again," and as the novel closes she is, for the moment at least, happy.

One might say the reader and/or the spectator has also gained new awareness. If we recognize and respond to Frankie's emotions, problems, and needs, we do so because these are universal — that is, archetypal. We may not ourselves have been victims of psychic inflation or had dual mothers, yet these and the other archetypal conditions and images in the novel are not alien to us, for they are buried deep in our collective psyches. McCullers shows the completion of a cycle of growth for one adolescent, and in doing so she illuminates a problem for our time—the need for collective balance and personal growth.

II

Having portrayed so well, in *The Member of the Wedding*, an adolescent's struggle for psychic growth, McCullers published a few years before her own death a novel about the second half of life, about a terminally ill man at the brink of middle age forced to confront his own mortality. McCullers had worked on her last novel, *Clock Without Hands* (1961), for many years, putting it away frequently, "only to resurrect it when the characters made sufficient demands." Finishing it was a kind of therapy for her (Carr 1975, pp. 486–487). The novel has particular relevance today, when so many are concerned about such fatal maladies as cancer, coronary disease, and AIDS, when all these and numerous other life-threatening illnesses get daily attention in the news media. I propose to examine *Clock Without Hands* not only from a Jungian point of view, but also from the viewpoint of today's leading thanatologist, Elizabeth Kübler-Ross. Jung himself declared that a doctor "must guard against falling into any specific, routine approach." He aimed to suit his analyses to the individual needs of his patients: "In one analysis I can be heard talking the Adlerian dialect, in another the Freudian" (1963, p. 131).[9]

Modern psychology has described death as a fulfillment of life and dying—for the terminally ill at least—as a rather well defined process, detailed by Kübler-Ross in *On Death and Dying*. McCullers, writing several years before Kübler-Ross, takes her character, J. T. Malone, through all five stages of dying, as outlined by Kübler-Ross, to a final fulfillment in death that can be interpreted in the light of Jung's ideas.

Clock Without Hands is concerned with several themes: racial relations and violence in the South, old age, adolescence, and in the words of one critic, "the isolated self in time" (Cook 1975, p. 116).[10] Central to all of these themes is the quality of "livingness" and the theme of death and dying. The two main characters, J. T. Malone and Judge Fox Clane, are dying throughout the novel, Malone from leukemia and Clane of old age and complications from a stroke. Two other characters, Grown Boy and Sherman Pew, also die, but they do not go through an extended process of dying. An off-stage character, John Clane, the judge's son, has committed suicide before the action of the novel begins. The judge is partly senile and too proud to admit his own mortality. J. T. Malone, on the other hand, is in the prime of life, a family man of thirty-nine with two growing children. The novel opens with his being handed, as it were, a death sentence: his doctor tells him he has leukemia and that he has only a year to fifteen months to live. The novel closes with Malone's death some fourteen months later.

It is Malone who, initially anyway, is "a man watching a clock without hands":

> For the first time he *knew* that death was near him. But the terror that choked him was not caused by the knowledge of his own death. The terror concerned some mysterious drama that was going on — although what the drama was about Malone did not know. (McCullers 1961, p. 25)

The "mysterious drama" is the process of dying and, ultimately, the process of individuation. Malone is terrified because he feels ignorant and helpless. His psyche is incomplete, undeveloped. The "clock without hands" is a mandala, an archetypal symbol that stands for both Malone's current incompleteness (the lack of hands) and his potential wholeness, a wholeness that the mandala as a complete circle portends. As Marie-Louise von Franz writes, "whenever man is confronted with something mysterious, unknown . . . his unconscious produces symbolic, mythical, that is, archetypal, models, which appear projected into the void. The same is also true, of course, with the mystery of death" (1986, p. xiii).

Literature has always treated the subject of death, but in Western culture the subject until recently has received short shrift in other quarters (save religion) because, as Kübler-Ross observes, "death has always been distasteful to man and will probably always be." Furthermore, she says, "in our unconscious, death is never possible in regard to ourselves. It is inconceivable for our unconscious to imagine an actual ending of our own life [sic] here on earth. . . . In simple terms, in our unconscious mind we can only be killed; it is inconceivable to die of a natural cause or of old age" (1969, p. 2).[11] The idea that one's own death is inconceivable is common to the three round characters who die or are dying in *Clock Without Hands* (Grown Boy is a flat character, symbolic of the random brutality of the South, of racial discrimination, and a catalyst to Jester Clane's growth.)

"Malone," McCullers tells us, "had never considered his own death except in some twilight, unreckoned future, or in terms of life insurance" (1961, p. 2). When his doctor tells him he has leukemia, Malone is already in the first stage of dying, that of denial and isolation: "He was unable to think about the months ahead or to imagine death. . . . he was unable to acknowledge the reality of approaching death" (ibid., pp. 8–9). Like Phillip Lovejoy in *The Square Root of Wonderful*, Malone is "surrounded by a zone of loneliness" (ibid., p. 8).[12]

Denial, common to most terminally ill patients both when initially told of their disease and in later stages of it, is "a healthy way of dealing with the uncomfortable and painful situation. . . . Denial functions as a buffer after unexpected shocking news, allows the patient to collect himself and, with time, mobilize other, less radical defenses" (Kübler-Ross 1969, p. 39). Thus, when Malone goes to Judge Clane to tell him of his illness and Clane deprecates medical doctors and advises Malone not to let them "intimidate" him, "Malone was comforted" and considered the likelihood that "a mistaken diagnosis" had been made (McCullers 1961, p. 16).

Judge Clane, himself half senile, has suffered a stroke and is slowly dying. Although he knows more about leukemia than he will admit to Malone (ibid., p. 184), he denies the possibility of his own death: "It was inconceivable to him that he would actually die" (ibid., p. 96). The judge also denies his stroke, at least in public. He

> would not admit it was a true stroke — spoke of "a light case of polio," "little seizure," etc. When he was up and around, he declared he used the walking stick because he liked it and that the "little attack" had probably benefited him as his mind had grown keener because of contemplation and "new studies." (Ibid., p. 56)

To the judge, denial is a strategy for living, a strategy Malone can use only sparingly, for he has a capacity to grow which the judge does not have.

Sherman Pew also lacks the capacity to grow. Unlike Grown Boy, he is intelligent and talented. He is a foil to Jester Clane, the sensitive grandson of Judge Clane. Born into the privileged white class, Jester is terrified of his own homosexual feelings toward Sherman, while deeply concerned about the plight of the blacks in the South. Sherman, an orphan black with blue eyes, is the victim of the worst manifestations of racial prejudice. Only toward the end of the novel do Sherman and Jester, separately, discover that Judge Clane had sentenced Sherman's black father to death for murdering the white husband of Sherman's white mother — an act done in self-defense. Jester's reaction to the discovery is to determine to become a lawyer, to follow in the footsteps of his father, John Clane, who had defended Sherman's father and who had committed suicide after the latter's execution. Sherman, on the other hand, feels the need to "*do something, do something, do something*" (ibid., p. 214). He tries various ways of defying segregation, but is not noticed until he moves into a white neighborhood.

Jester overhears a group of white bigots meeting at Malone's pharmacy. They make plans to bomb Sherman's house, and Jester quickly warns Sherman. The archetype of love moves Jester. McCullers implies this is a way of bringing harmony between black and white. But Sherman chooses martyrdom: "I am going to stay right here. Right here. Bombing or no." His martyr complex is actually a denial of the possibility of his own dying. His decision is irrational, however much he is in the right: "All I know is, I have rented this house, paid my money, and I am going to stay" (ibid., p. 229).

As I showed in the chapter on *The Picture of Dorian Gray*, scapegoatism is, from the Jungian viewpoint, the projection of the shadow by the people who scapegoat onto the scapegoat. The bigoted white men who kill Sherman project their own inferior personalities – the archetype of the shadow – onto Sherman and all blacks. Rather than come to terms with their own defects of character, which they fear and would prefer not to acknowledge even slightly, they accuse their victims of these defects, creating thus a false rationale to persecute and murder. Victimizing a scapegoat makes them feel a false sense of superiority. When Jester, intending to kill him, offers Sammy Lank, the man who threw the bomb that killed Sherman, a plane ride, Sammy thinks: "Already I'm such a famous man in town that Jester Clane takes me for an airplane ride" (ibid., pp. 231–232). Jester, in a moment of compassion, takes the gun he had brought to kill Sammy and drops it out of the plane.

The second stage of dying is that of "anger, rage, envy, and resentment." The anger is "displaced in all directions and projected onto the environment at times almost at random" (Kübler-Ross 1969, p. 50). It is not surprising, then, that when Malone is faced with telling his wife, whom he has not loved in years, about his disease, he feels "terror and alarm . . . exasperated and horrified," especially when after telling her, she refers to sex (McCullers 1961, pp. 46–47). The five stages of dying are not mutually exclusive: they overlap (Kübler-Ross 1969, p. 263), and from time to time throughout his illness until the final stage of acceptance Malone feels anger and rage. "Malone's whole being was outraged," for example, because the doctor had not suggested "the faintest cure" (McCullers 1961, p. 114), just as today, AIDS patients are understandably enraged that the Food and Drug Administration is so slow to approve new drugs for treating the disease, even though there is at present no cure for AIDS. A simple question from his wife ("Aren't you feeling well, Hon?") provokes severe anger:

> Rage made Malone fist his hands until the knuckles whitened. A man with leukemia not feeling well? What the hell did the woman think he had . . . chicken pox or spring fever? (Ibid., pp. 120–121)

But he suppresses his rage and merely answers: "I feel no better nor no worse than I deserve" (ibid., p. 121).

In a final vain attempt at denial, Malone goes to Johns Hopkins for a new diagnosis, and when the familiar verdict is returned he is "sick with rage." Again he clenches his fists until the knuckles are white. He is frequently "subject to these fits of sudden rage" (ibid., p. 209). The rage is mixed with denial:

> He could not think directly of his own death because it was unreal to him. But these rages, unprovoked and surprising even to himself, stormed frequently in his once calm heart. (Ibid., p. 209)

Yet the anger provides no relief. He is left with a kind of existential dread, "the feeling that something awful and incomprehensible was going to happen that he was powerless to prevent" (ibid., p. 210).

The third stage, bargaining, is an attempt "to postpone the inevitable happening" (Kübler-Ross 1969, p. 82). In the bargaining is "an implicit promise that the patient will not ask for more if this one postponement is granted" (ibid., p. 84). Bargaining for Malone takes two forms. Because the judge had told him to eat liver to improve his blood, Malone, who hates liver of any kind, eats it every morning (McCullers 1961, pp. 113–114). The other form of Malone's bargaining is closer to Kübler-Ross's description. He wishes to go alone to Vermont or Maine so that he may again see snow. The thought of snow reminds him of freedom and of the guilt provoked by the only time he had committed adultery years before. Malone is, as it were, bargaining to "sin" once more before he dies. He never has the opportunity.

I have referred to the dread that Malone experiences. Every morning of his last summer he awakes with "an amorphous dread" (McCullers 1961, p. 113). He is in the fourth stage of dying, depression, which Kübler-

Ross calls "a stepping-stone towards final acceptance" (1969, p. 263). The depression is the result of "a sense of great loss" (ibid., p. 85), either a reaction to a loss in the past or one to come. Malone experiences this kind of depression while in the hospital when he picks up a copy of Kierkegaard's *Sickness unto Death* and is deeply impressed by the following passage:

> *The greatest danger, that of losing one's own self, may pass*
> *off quietly as if it were nothing; every other loss, that of an*
> *arm, a leg, five dollars, a wife, etc., is sure to be noticed.*
> (McCullers 1961, p. 147)

Normally Malone would have paid no attention to these words. But having an incurable disease, he is "chilled" by the words. And he broods about his past, his loveless life, for "dying had quickened his livingness" (ibid., p. 149).

The night the lynch meeting is held at his pharmacy Malone looks at the May moon "with a hollow sadness," wondering if it would be the last moon he would see (ibid., p. 220). He is ready for a transformation from depression to acceptance. As soon as he sees that instead of "leading citizens" the group is composed mostly of "nameless . . . halfway liquored up" men passing a bottle around, he regrets having allowed the meeting to be held at his pharmacy (ibid., p. 221). Like the barber in Faulkner's "Dry September," Malone is the only white man at the meeting to speak up for reason and decency. (Jester is witness to the meeting, but not a participant. He rushes to warn Sherman of the impending bombing.) The men draw lots to decide who will do the bombing. The lot falls on Malone, who declines: "I am too near death to sin, to murder. . . . I don't want to endanger my soul" (ibid., pp. 224–225). Because of his dying Malone is able to redeem himself: he abstains from evil.

Throughout his dying Malone has never lost hope, and this is typical of the terminally ill patients about whom Kübler-Ross writes (1969, p. 138). But there comes a time when the inevitable must be accepted calmly, "an existence without fear and despair" (ibid., p. 120). McCullers describes Malone's acceptance of death thus:

> Yes, the earth had revolved its seasons and spring had come
> again. But there was no longer a revulsion against nature,
> against things. A strange lightness had come upon his soul
> and he exalted. He looked at nature now and it was a part of

> himself. He was no longer a man watching a clock without
> hands. He was not alone, he did not rebel, he did not suffer.
> He did not even think of death these days. He was not a man
> dying . . . nobody died, everybody died. (1961, p. 236)

Furthermore, the archetype of love has asserted its healing power: he loves his wife again, and "he was possessed by a strange euphoria . . . in dying, living assumed order and a simplicity that Malone had never known before" (ibid., pp. 238 and 241). In the words of Kübler-Ross, in death "we are going back to the stage that we started out with and the circle of life is closed" (1969, p. 120). In accepting his own death, in loving his wife again, Malone has achieved a wholeness symbolized by the clock, "the circle of life."

The stages of dying I have discussed and applied to J. T. Malone are characteristic of terminally ill patients, but the need to accept death is universal. Kübler-Ross speaks of the need we all have of "facing and accepting the reality of our own death [sic]" (1969, p. 18). And Jungian critic Alex Aronson points out that "the process of healing includes an acceptance of the phenomenon of dying as part of the process of living" (1972, p. 34).

On the unconscious level, Malone has achieved what Jung calls individuation, the integration of the Self. In his decision to rise above violence against Sherman Pew, he has conquered his own shadow — the beast within. His wife, from whom he had been estranged for most of his marriage in spite of the fact they had continued to live together, is symbolic of the contrasexual, the anima; and in loving her again he has achieved as much of a union with the anima as he can.

Jung believes that death can be "a joyful event. In the light of eternity, it is a wedding, a *mysterium coniunctionis*. The soul attains, as it were, its missing half, it achieves wholeness" (1963, p. 314). This is why Malone finds nature a "part of himself," why he feels "a strange euphoria," and why life "assumed order." In death he achieves a psychic unity he had not known in life, and that is why he dies at peace, "without struggle or fear" (McCullers 1961, p. 241).

McCullers was fond of quoting Terence: "Nothing human is alien to me" (1971, p. 314). Death is as much a part of being human as is birth. In her personal life McCullers was well acquainted with sickness, death, and dying. In her last novel, with an intuitive knowledge of these themes characteristic of the finest literary artists, she created another myth for our time.

Notes

1. Because so many Pisceans lived there (George Davis, W. H. Auden, and McCullers herself), Anaïs Nin, who visited the house in 1943, dubbed it "February House" (Carr 1975, p. 130). Among the other residents who lived there at various times were Gypsy Rose Lee, Louis MacNeice, Benjamin Britten, Peter Pears, Richard Wright, and his wife, Ellen Poppell (ibid., pp. 118–127).

2. See also Carr (1975), who notes that as McCullers and Lee "walked silently back to the house, Carson was trembling. She was certain now of the style and theme of her book. Its focus had sharpened at last" (p. 121).

3. This description is from the play version. In the play, Berenice is "about forty-five," but in the novel she has been saying she's thirty-five for "at least three years." In the play, John Henry is seven.

4. In the play version, she is described as "a dreamy, restless girl, and periods of energetic activity alternative with a rapt attention to her inward world of fantasy" (McCullers 1951a, p. 1).

5. Frank Baldanza, examining the similarity of the ideas of Plato to those of McCullers, points out that in *The Member of the Wedding*, "love is synonymous, almost mathematically, with wholeness" (1958, p. 160).

6. Tristram and Iseult, in Swinburne's version of the legend, are an example of Ideal Love (see Chapter Three, pp. 49, 66). Baldanza has shown how Berenice's relationship with Ludie Freeman and her search for another Ludie after Ludie's death resembles Plato's theory of love in the *Symposium* (1958, pp. 159–160).

7. Her "crimes" are not all that unusual for a girl her age: "She took the pistol from her father's bureau drawer and carried it all over town and shot up the cartridges in a vacant lot. She changed into a robber and stole a three-way knife. . . . One Saturday in May she committed a secret and unknown sin. In the MacKean's garage, with Barney MacKean, they committed a queer sin, and how bad it was she did not know" (McCullers 1946, p. 626).

8. Perhaps significantly, McCullers herself, who struggled for five years to write *The Member of the Wedding*, "felt certain that her inability to proceed well with *The Bride* [an early title of the novel] was symptomatic of her greater spiritual loss . . . a loss of God and godliness which haunted her, intermittently, much of her life" (Carr 1975, p. 194).

9. One of the foremost Jungian analysts, Marie-Louise von Franz, acknowledges Kübler-Ross's work in her own book, *On Dreams and Death* (1986, pp. vii and 62). Kübler-Ross provides the highly laudatory blurb for the Shambhala paperback edition of von Franz's book.

10. Evans writes: "The search for self is the theme" of *Clock Without Hands*. He adds that "indeed, the 'existential crisis' — the achievement of identity through engagement and choice — is at the very centre of the narrative" (1965, p. 173).

11. Von Franz, however, suggests that for the old and the terminally ill, the unconscious produces dreams which prepare the individual for "impending death" (1986, p. viii).

12. Complaining, Lovejoy uses the same words: "I feel surrounded by a zone of loneliness" (McCullers 1958, p. 48).

Works Cited

Aronson, Alex. 1972. *Psyche and Symbol in Shakespeare*. Bloomington, Ind.: Indiana University Press.

Baldanza, Frank. 1958. Plato in Dixie. *The Georgia Review* 12:151–167.

Carr, Virginia Spencer. 1975. *The Lonely Hunter: A Biography of Carson McCullers*. Garden City, N.Y.: Doubleday.

Cook, Richard M. 1975. *Carson McCullers*. New York: Frederick Ungar.

Evans, Oliver. 1965. *The Ballad of Carson McCullers: A Biography*. New York: Coward-McCann.

Fordham, Frieda. 1966. *An Introduction to Jung's Psychology*. Harmondsworth, England: Penguin.

Graver, Lawrence. 1969. *Carson McCullers*. Minneapolis: University of Minnesota Press.

Jacobi, Jolande. 1968. *The Psychology of C. G. Jung: An Introduction with Illustrations*. Trans. Ralph Manheim, trans. New Haven, Conn.: Yale University Press.

Jung, C. G. 1926. Spirit and life. *CW* 8:319–337. Princeton, N.J.: Princeton University Press, 1960.

———. 1936–1937. The concept of the collective unconscious. *CW* 9i:42–53. Princeton, N.J.: Princeton University Press, 1959.

———. 1950. A study in the process of individuation. *CW* 9i:290–354. Princeton, N.J.: Princeton University Press, 1959.

———. 1963. *Memories, Dreams, Reflections*. Richard and Clara Winston, trans. Aniela Jaffé, ed. New York: Vintage.

Jung, C. G., and Kerényi, C. 1963. *Essays on a Science of Mythology: The Myth of the Divine Child and the Mysteries of Eleusis*. R. F. C. Hull, trans. Princeton, N.J.: Princeton University Press.

Kübler-Ross, Elisabeth. 1969. *On Death and Dying*. New York: MacMillan.

McCullers, Carson. 1951. *The Ballad of the Sad Café: The Novels and Stories of Carson McCullers*. Boston: Houghton.

_____. 1951a. *The Member of the Wedding*. New York: New Directions.

_____. 1958. *The Square Root of Wonderful*. Boston: Houghton.

_____. 1961. *Clock Without Hands*. Boston: Houghton.

_____. 1971. *The Mortgaged Heart*. Margarita G. Smith, ed. Boston: Houghton.

McDowell, Margaret B. 1980. *Carson McCullers*. Boston: Twayne.

van der Post, Laurens. 1975. *Jung and the Story of Our Time*. New York: Vintage.

Vickery, John B. 1960. Carson McCullers: a map of love. *Wisconsin Studies in Contemporary Literature* 1:13–24.

von Franz, Marie-Louise. 1986. *On Dreams and Death: A Jungian Interpretation*. Emmanuel Xipolitas Kennedy and Vernon Brooks, trans. Boston: Shambhala.

Wikborg, Eleanor. 1975. *Carson McCullers' "The Member of the Wedding": Aspects of Structure and Style*. Göteborg, Sweden: Acta Universitatis Gothoburgensis.

Chapter Seven

The Archetype of Love
in the Age of Anxiety:
W. H. Auden*

But in my arms till break of day
Let the living creature lie,
Mortal, guilty, but to me
The entirely beautiful.
                    W. H. Auden, "Lullaby"

I

Of all the authors I examine at length in this study, W. H. Auden is the only one we can be sure wrote with a conscious awareness of Jung's ideas. Auden appended to his 1935 article, "Psychology and Art To-day," a list of "Books To Read." Two works by Jung are included on the list: *Psychology of the Unconscious* and *Two Essays in [sic] Analytical Psychology* (Callan 1983, p. 269).[1] Auden's most famous long poem, *The Age of Anxiety* (1947), is informed by Jungian ideas; indeed, each of its four characters represents one of the functions of consciousness: Malin stands for thinking; Rosetta for feeling; Quant for intuition; and Emble for sensation (Callan 1965, p. 155; and Fuller 1970, p. 189). Freud is generally considered chief among the psychological influences on Auden, but John Fuller's analysis of *The Age of Anxiety*(1970, pp. 188–201) and other recent studies suggest that Jung is perhaps as important an influence.[2]

Auden described himself as a "thinking-intuitive" type (Mendelson 1981, p. xxii), and these two functions, thinking and intuition, are precisely the ones most necessary to the writing of poetry. He is, however, most known for his catholic intellect and is hardly the type of poet whose

*Portions of this chapter were first published as "Auden's Quest Poems: 'Lady Weeping at the Crossroads' and 'Atlantis' " in *American Imago*, vol. 39, no. 2 (1982), © 1982 by Wayne State University Press, Detroit, Michigan 48202. Reprinted with permission.

creative process one would expect to correspond to Jungian theory.[3] Not a romantic in the traditional sense of the word, he does not pour out his heart in personal effusions, nor does he use a great deal of natural imagery. Of the great nineteenth-century romantic poets, Auden most resembles Byron, and Byron himself harks back to eighteenth-century satire and rationalism. Christopher Isherwood, in "Some Notes on Auden's Early Poetry" (1937), says Auden tried "to regard things 'clinically,' as he called it. . . .Colours and smells were condemned as romantic: Form alone was significant" (p. 13). Yet if Auden was "essentially a scientist," Isherwood writes, he was also "a musician and a ritualist . . . [and] a Scandinavian" brought up on Icelandic sagas (ibid., p. 10); so that from an early age he was influenced by the world of myth—in the high Anglican rituals of his childhood (and what are rituals but reenactments of myth?) and in the myths of Iceland, which eventually he helped translate into English (with Paul B. Taylor and Peter H. Salus) in *The Elder Edda* (1969) (see Carpenter 1981, p. 429).

Some of Auden's ideas about creativity echo Jung's neo-Platonic idea: "Art is a kind of innate drive that seizes a human being and makes him its instrument" (Jung 1950, p. 101). When he was young (age twenty-five), Auden wrote to sixteen-year-old John Cornford, whose English teacher had sent Auden a poem by Cornford: "Real poetry originates in the guts and only flowers in the head." At the same time he recommended "that you might do more with stricter verse forms" (quoted by Osborne 1979, pp. 95–96). To John Pudney, who also sent poems, Auden wrote: "Never write from your head, write from your cock" (quoted by Carpenter 1981, p. 118). At the age of twenty, he wrote to Bill McElwee: "Writing must be like shitting, one's sole feeling that of a natural function properly performed, and I get excited about it" (quoted by Carpenter 1981, p. 158). Auden's biographer, Humphrey Carpenter, comments that the "self-consciousness" revealed here "grew out of the fact that he [Auden] lived through his intellect rather than his emotions" (ibid.). About eight years later, in the introduction to *The Poet's Tongue* (1935), an anthology edited by Auden and John Garrett, Auden defined poetry as "memorable speech." Poetry "must move our emotions, or excite our intellect" (Auden 1977, p. 327). Furthermore, "the test of a poet is the frequency and diversity of the occasions on which we remember his poetry" (ibid., pp. 327–328). A. L. Rowse, who knew Auden at Oxford, notes "Auden's life-long practice of writing poetry as an act of will," which Rowse sees as a practice conflicting with poetry which "arises from the deepest sources within one" (1987, p. 34). Auden's ideas about creativity and his practice of writing poetry, then, would seem to be inconsistent, or at least some-what contradictory.[4]

While it is true that Auden's poetry "is not often emotionally demon-strative" (Fuller 1970, p. 8), this does not mean the emotion is not there. The emotion, when it exists, is highly controlled by the thinking function. Often, even in Auden's love lyrics, we find intellect warring with emotion, as if the conscious thinking function were struggling to control spontane-ous emotions and images from the unconscious. Those poems which have had the greatest impact are those which appeal in a visionary way, those which have a collective appeal because they stir something compensatory in the collective unconscious. In this chapter I propose to discuss a few of these poems, which may or may not have been written with Jung in mind, and then to discuss two of Auden's shorter but important quest poems, written not long after his move to the United States in January 1939 and his reembrace of Christianity, poems that more clearly than the others are informed by Jungian ideas.

II

Auden's poem, "In Memory of Sigmund Freud" (November 1939), is kinder to Freud, who had died in September 1939, than Jung's essay with the same title (Jung 1939).[5] Of course, Jung and Freud had long been estranged from each other after Jung, who had been Freud's disciple, formulated his own psychology. Auden had no such obstacle to objectivity. Both acknowledge Freud's immense influence on contemporary culture. "The Freudian outlook," says Jung, "has affected practically every sphere of our contemporary thinking, except that of the exact sciences" (1939, p. 41). To Auden, Freud "is no more a person . . . but a whole climate of opinion / Under whom we conduct our differing lives" (Auden 1979, p. 93). In an understated but characteristic phrase of "memorable speech," Auden calls Freud "An important Jew who died in exile" (ibid., p. 92) and who unwillingly was going to miss the coming international conflict ("So many plausible young futures" (ibid., p. 91)). Auden is as capable of overstatement as he is of understatement: Freud "wasn't clever at all" (ibid., p. 92). Jung is more explicit: "By training he [Freud] was no psychi-atrist, no psychologist, and no philosopher. In philosophy he lacked even the most rudimentary elements of education. He once assured me person-ally that it had never occurred to him to read Nietzsche" (1939, p. 41). Perhaps Auden was unaware of Freud's ignorance. In his 1935 essay, "Psy-chology and Art To-day," Auden divides the "Christian era into three periods . . . the third just beginning" (1977, p. 337). "Freud," Auden says, "belongs to the third of these phases, which in the sphere of psychology may be said to have begun with Nietzsche" (ibid., p. 339).

Nevertheless, Auden freely recognizes Freud's faults: "the autocratic pose / The paternal strictness" (1979, p. 93). Unlike poetry, which in the more famous elegy, "In Memory of W. B. Yeats," Auden declared "makes nothing happen" (1979, p. 82), Freudian psychology "can only hinder or help, /, The proud can still be proud but find it / A little harder, and the tyrant tries / To make him do but doesn't care for him much" (ibid., p. 93). Jung would probably agree that Freud "quietly surrounds all our habits of growth." But Jung would, I think, disagree that Freud taught us "To be enthusiastic over the night . . .because it needs our love" (ibid., p. 94). Jung saw Freud as a necessary corrective to nineteenth-century optimism ("All that gush about man's innate goodness"), if not a prophet, "a prophetic figure. Like Nietzsche, he overthrew the gigantic idols of our day" (Jung 1939, p. 46). Auden seems to recognize this too, for Freud, Auden says, "showed us what evil is." Furthermore:

> No wonder the ancient cultures of conceit
> In his technique of unsettlement foresaw
> The fall of princes, the collapse of
> Their lucrative patterns of frustration.
>
> (Ibid., p. 93)

Unfortunately, Jung writes, "Nowhere does he [Freud] break through to a vision of the helpful, healing powers which would let the unconscious be of some benefit to the patient." To Jung, "there is no illness that is not at the same time an unsuccessful attempt at a cure" (1939, p. 46). Hence his belief in the compensatory power of archetypal images.

Speaking from their "personal friendship which bound me to Freud for many years . . . [and which] permitted a deep glimpse into the mind of this remarkable man," Jung declares: "He was a man possessed by a daemon—a man who had been vouchsafed an overwhelming revelation that took possession of his soul and never let him go" (1939, p. 48). Perhaps this accounts for the "autocratic pose" and the "paternal strictness" which "Clung to his utterance and features" (Auden 1979, p. 93). Still, Auden sees Freud as offering more healing than Jung grants Freud.

Freud, Auden recognizes, had made the individual of utmost importance: "If he [Freud] succeeded, why, the Generalized Life / Would become impossible." Auden concludes:

One rational voice is dumb: over a grave
The household of Impulse mourns one dearly loved.
    Sad is Eros, builder of cities,
    And weeping anarchic Aphrodite.

(Ibid., p. 95)

Auden here echoes Freud's own words, which Auden quoted in his essay on psychology and art:

> We may insist as often as we please that the human intellect is powerless when compared with the impulses of man, and we may be right in what we say. All the same there is something peculiar about this weakness. The voice of the intellect is soft and low, but it is persistent and continues until it has secured a hearing. After what may be countless repetitions, it does get a hearing. This is one of the few facts which may help to make us rather more hopeful about the future of mankind. (1977, p. 342)

Strangely enough, Auden uses this quotation to support his own assertion about "parable-art" (the kind of art opposed to "escape-art"), "that art which shall teach man to unlearn hatred and learn love" (ibid., pp. 341–342). Here again we have a central conflict in Auden — that between intellect and emotion.

Unlike Freud, who seems to allow no place for the spirit, both Auden and Jung do. For Auden, it was love which would bring the healing. "In the deserts of the heart / Let the healing fountain start," he writes (1979, p. 83). I agree with Stephen Spender that Auden's poetry is, basically, about "the central need of love." If the "symptoms have to be diagnosed," the "cure" is love:

> At one time Love, in the sense of Freudian release from inhibition; at another time a vaguer and more exalted idea of loving; at still another the Social Revolution; and at a yet later stage, Christianity. Essentially the direction of Auden's poetry has been towards the defining of the concept of Love. (Spender 1953, p. 28)

I suggest also that, for Auden, love is an archetype of great compensatory power, whatever name, Eros or Agape, he may attach to it.

    The poem which begins "Lay your sleeping head, my love, / Human on my faithless arm" (January 1937) has powerful emotions carefully controlled by intellect. Originally the poem had no title. Later Auden called it "Lullaby" (1966, p. 107). It is without a doubt his most famous love poem. Jack Kroll chose to begin his obituary of Auden in *Newsweek* with the first stanza of "Lullaby" (1973, p. 117); and Timothy Foote, in *Time* magazine's obituary, called it "one of the most beautiful love lyrics ever written" (1973, p. 113). Fuller calls it "perhaps the most well-known of Auden's lyrics" (1970, p. 116). Why does this poem have such a powerful and broad appeal? The Jungian answer is that the poem speaks to our collective unconscious in a compensatory way. In it Auden found, as he did in so many of his other poems, "the language for a vision of man in his wholeness and integrity" (Kroll 1973, p. 117). One of Auden's executors, his editor and biographer, Edward Mendelson, gives another reason for the poem's appeal and importance: "It is the first English poem in which a lover proclaims, in moral terms and during a shared night of love, his own faithlessness" (1981, p. 233).

Here is the complete first stanza:

> Lay your sleeping head, my love,
> Human on my faithless arm;
> Time and fevers burn away
> Individual beauty from
> Thoughtful children, and the grave
> Proves the child ephemeral:
> But in my arms till break of day
> Let the living creature lie,
> Mortal, guilty, but to me
> The entirely beautiful.

(Auden 1979, p. 50)

The poem, written when Auden was almost thirty, was, as Auden's first biographer says, "addressed to a teenage boy" (Osborne 1979, p. 140), but its appeal is clearly universal and Auden wrote it during a time when prejudice against homosexuals was even stronger than it is today, so that his concealment of the sex of the beloved is not surprising.[6]

Love in this poem operates as a great unifier of opposites, even if the union is only temporary: "Soul and body have no bounds" during the moment of sexual union (Auden 1979, p. 50). Although Mendelson disagrees (1981, pp. 231–232), I tend to agree with Fuller's comment on the second stanza: it "proposes that on the one hand Eros can lead to Agape." However, I disagree with Fuller's corresponding idea that "on the other

[hand] . . . 'abstract insight' can induce Eros: the lover and the desert saint are closer than they might appear" (1970, p. 116). Auden writes:

> Grave the vision Venus sends
> Of supernatural sympathy,
> Universal love and hope;
> While an abstract insight wakes
> Among the glaciers and the rocks
> The hermit's sensual ecstacy.

(1979, p. 50)

The hermit, presumably, is alone. His "sensual ecstasy" therefore must be mystical experience, comparable to what the Hindus call *samadhi*, a union with God that transcends the body but takes place nevertheless within the body and is experienced as "ecstacy."

The third stanza places the two lovers' experience within a collective context. While recognizing that "Certainty, fidelity / On the stroke of midnight pass / Like vibrations of a bell," the speaker also recognizes that "fashionable madmen raise / Their pedantic boring cry" (Auden 1979, p. 51). The "cost" which the "dreaded cards foretell" is not only the cost of infidelity on the speaker's part, but also the cost of the "madmen" who are about to cause a great collective disruption in the world at large. The poem emphasizes the value of the moment: "but from this night / Not a whisper, not a thought, / Not a kiss nor look be lost" (ibid., p. 51).

The "involuntary powers"—Venus and her son Eros—the speaker invokes in the final stanza are barriers against the forces of the unconscious mentioned in the previous stanza. These forces, the "madmen," are symbolic of the collective shadow then threatening the world, personified by such dictators as Franco, Hitler, and Mussolini. Despite the frank recognition that the love will pass, the poem's message is that love can reconcile the opposites of the "day of sweetness" the lover wishes for the beloved and the "Nights of insult" which threaten their love. This archetypal love is the only answer, the corrective as it were, to the brutality of the larger, collective world.

In this context, it may be well to note what Auden said in an essay published some eleven years later as the introduction to yet another book he edited, *The Portable Greek Reader* (1948) and reprinted as "The Greeks and Us" in *Forewords and Afterwords* (1973). Auden points out that romantic heterosexual love as we think of it was unknown before the twelfth century. However, in Plato "we find descriptions of something like what we mean by romantic love spoken of with approval" (Auden 1973, p. 22). The differences are that

> this kind of love is only possible in a homosexual relation . . . [and] it is only approved of as the necessary first stage in the growth of the soul. The ultimate good is the love of the impersonal as universal good; the best thing that could happen to a man would be that he should fall in love with the Good immediately, but owing to the fact that his soul is entangled in matter and time, he can only get there by degrees; first he falls in love with a beautiful individual, then he can progress to love of beauty in general, then to love of justice, and so on. (Ibid., pp. 22–23)[7]

Heterosexuals find attaining this kind of Platonic love more difficult than homosexuals because the relationship between heterosexuals

> leads beyond itself, not to the universal, but to more individuals, namely the love of and responsibility for a family, whereas, in the homosexual case . . . the love which it has aroused is free to develop in any direction the lovers choose, and that direction should be towards wisdom which, once acquired, will enable them to teach human beings procreated in the normal way how to become a good society. (Ibid., p. 23)

What procreation in other than a "normal way" is Auden does not say. But he adds: "For love is to be judged by its social and political value" (ibid.).

This is the sort of love "Lullaby" aims at, but Auden was honest enough to admit that the future of the particular two lovers he writes about did not bode well because of the speaker's infidelity and other threats to their relationship. As Mendelson writes, "In Auden's view, poetry could not be exempted from ethical standards of truth or falsehood: a poem could be a lie, and what was more serious, a poetic lie could be more persuasive in the public realm than lies less eloquently expressed" (Auden 1979, p. xix). If the relationship he was writing about was temporary, by his own standards he had to say so. Many years later, he was to write "The More Loving One" (September 1957), which contains the following famous couplet:

If equal affection cannot be,
Let the more loving one be me.

(Auden 1979, p. 237)

If this is the "truth about love" he longed to know, he was willing to embrace it, no matter how short of Ideal Love it might be (Auden 1966, p. 95). Whatever personal reasons inspired the lines (his relationship with Chester Kallman was the likely inspiration), it was the archetype of love he expressed, the central archetype of his collected poetry.

Contrary to what Auden said in his elegy for Yeats about poetry making nothing happen, Auden came to believe, as Mendelson writes, that "words had the potential to do good or evil, whether their source was political discourse or the ordered images of a poem" (Auden 1979, p. xix). And, as we have seen, Auden felt "a poetic lie could be more persuasive in the public realm than lies less eloquently expressed." This is why he rejected another of his own most famous poems (he felt it was dishonest), "September 1, 1939" (ibid., pp. 86–89). As Mendelson's inclusion of "September 1, 1939" in the Selected Poems shows, many readers disagree with Auden's rejection of the poem from his canon. Again, as a Jungian critic I would say the reason the poem continues to appeal to so many readers, apart from its obvious prosodic merits, is that it has an extraordinary appeal to the collective unconscious. It contains Auden's most famous line: "We must love one another or die." This is the line about which E. M. Forster commented: "Because he once wrote 'We must love one another or die,' he can command me to follow him" (quoted by Mendelson 1981, p. 326). Auden later decided the line was a "damned lie," changed it to "We must love one another and die," and finally abandoned the poem altogether (see Mendelson 1981, pp. 324–330 for a full history and a different interpretation of the poem).

As he does in "Lullaby," Auden speaks in "September 1, 1939" with both a personal and a public voice; he begins with the personal, makes a collective application, and ends with the personal. At the end of "a low dishonest decade" and on the day Hitler invaded Poland, thus beginning World War II, the speaker of the poem sits "in one of the dives / On Fifty-Second Street." What Jung says of archetypal images applies here: "they give form to countless typical experiences of our ancestors. They are, so to speak, the psychic residua of innumerable experiences of the same type" (1931, p. 81). The archetypal shadow has appeared again:

> Accurate scholarship can
> Unearth the whole offence
> From Luther until now
> That has driven a culture mad,
> Find what occurred at Linz,
> What huge imago made
> A psychopathic god:
> I and the public know
> What all schoolchildren learn,
> Those to whom evil is done
> Do evil in return.
>
> (Auden 1979, p. 86)

Hitler, who was born in Linz, symbolized the shadow collectively for Germany, which had projected this archetype from the collective unconscious onto him. Post–World War I Germans wanted order and power without realizing that, as Jung writes, Hitler "symbolized something in every individual." Jung goes on:

> He [Hitler] was the most prodigious personification of all human inferiorities. He was an utterly incapable, unadapted, irresponsible, psychopathic personality, full of empty, infantile fantasies, but cursed with the keen intuition of a rat or a guttersnipe. He represented the shadow, the inferior part of everybody's personality, in an overwhelming degree, and this was another reason why they fell for him. (1946, p. 223)

"The strength of Collective Man" is a mockery when "Imperialism's face / And the international wrong" are all that result from the "euphoric dream" of a people who have not accommodated the shadow within themselves (Auden 1979, p. 87).

Auden understands that Eros is not enough to combat such collective evil:

138

For the error bred in the bone
Of each woman and each man
Craves what it cannot have,
Not universal love
But to be loved alone.

(Ibid., p. 88)

People, the "commuters" and the "helpless governors," cling to their personae, their public roles in life, without understanding that Agape, the selfless love of others, is what is needed now.[8]

Hunger allows no choice
To the citizen or the police;
We must love one another or die.

(Ibid., p. 88)

What can the poet do but offer "a voice"? So he concludes:

Defenceless under the night
Our world in stupor lies;
Yet, dotted everywhere,
Ironic points of light
Flash out wherever the Just
Exchange their messages:
May I, composed like them
Of Eros and of dust,
Beleaguered by the same
Negation and despair,
Show an affirming flame.

(Ibid., p. 89)

In his introduction to *The Poet's Tongue* (1935), Auden had written: "poetry can appeal to every level of consciousness" (1977, p. 329). In "September 1, 1939," the situation and setting, the rhetoric, and the images appeal to the conscious mind. The archetypal symbols and patterns—the shadow, love (Eros and Agape), the building up of forces (hunger, apathy, idealistic and demagogic talk by politicians about democracy and authority) that result in an uprising from the collective unconscious of the collective shadow—all these appeal to the collective unconscious in a compensatory way, a way intended to correct contemporary imbalance.

And all these symbols and patterns are as relevant today as they were in 1939. Indeed, they have never stopped being relevant. Despite his "disillusionment with political protest poetry" (Osborne 1979, p. 289), something in his unconscious moved Auden to protest by writing a poem, "August 1968," against the Soviet occupation of Czechoslovakia in August 1968:

> The Ogre does what ogres can,
> Deeds quite impossible for Man,
> But one prize is beyond his reach,
> The Ogre cannot master Speech:
> About a subjugated plain,
> Among its desperate and slain,
> The Ogre stalks with hands on hips,
> While drivel gushes from his lips.

> (1979, p. 291)

The collective shadow once again had forced its image not only upon the world but also into one of Auden's poems. Unlike "September 1, 1939," "August 1968" offers the image only, not a solution. In one of his final poems, "Archaeology" (August 1973), Auden recognizes the shadow element in the making of history:

> From Archaeology
> one moral, at least, may be drawn,
> to wit, that all

> our text-books lie.
> What they call History
> is nothing to vaunt of,

> being made, as it is,
> by the criminal in us . . .

> (1979, p. 304)

Lest this seem pessimistic, Auden adds: "goodness is timeless." For Auden the way to goodness is always the way of love.

III

In 1961 Auden stated: "The persistent appeal of the Quest as a literary form is due, I believe, to its validity as a symbolic description of our subjective personal experience of existence as historical. . . . the Quest tale is ill adapted to subtle portrayals of characters; its personages are almost bound to be Archetypes rather than idiosyncratic individuals" (1961, pp. 82 and 86). The quest is one of Auden's favorite motifs, and I would like now to examine two of Auden's shorter but important quest poems: "Lady Weeping at the Crossroads" (1940) and "Atlantis" (January 1941). (For a Jungian interpretation of "The Quest," see Long 1974.) In these poems, Auden draws on archetype, fairy tale, and myth to illustrate aspects of the modern personal search for what Jung calls individuation.

The ballad, "Lady Weeping at the Crossroads," is in the second person: the speaker directly addresses the heroine, who as the title and the first line indicate, is at a place of decision, "the crossroads." The speaker asks a rhetorical question:

> Would you meet your love
> In the twilight with his greyhounds,
> And the hawk on his glove?
>
> (Auden 1979, p. 95)

At first, in archetypal terms, one is tempted to assume the lady's task is to integrate her ego with the animus (her "love") — the unconscious "masculine" part of a woman's psyche. But the penultimate stanza clearly indicates that the task involved in the poem is not the coming to terms with the animus but rather the coming to terms with the shadow, one's own hidden inner being: "See yourself at last" (ibid.).[9]

In the process of individuation, as we have seen, meeting and accommodating the shadow is necessary before accommodation of the contrasexual, the anima for a man, the animus for a woman, can occur. The lady in Auden's poem is, until the last stanza, successful in all the tasks with which she is charged. She must "Stare the hot sun out of heaven" (symbolizing the harshness of consciousness) "That the night may come" (that is, the unconscious, where she can further her individual quest) (ibid.). As the lady proceeds on her mission, we see that she will stop at nothing to achieve her goal, and hence her shadow personality is subtly revealed. The tone of the poem is objective, almost cruel, and coupled with the use of the second person and the renaissance setting, enables the poet to keep a safe personal distance from his material — the thinking function is firmly in control.

The lady is told to make the traditional descent into hell ("Wear out patience in the lowest / Dungeons of the sea"), another indication that the major task is accommodation with the unconscious. She must find "the golden key" which will provide the essential self-knowledge. A Charon-like figure ("the / Dread guard") is watching the threshold, waiting to be bribed "with a kiss."

On the other side of "the abyss" is the "deserted castle," a frequent symbol for the psyche. It is "Ready to explore," and ironically "Doubt and danger" seem "past." The lady finds there is no love to meet. Instead, she must meet herself, and the speaker tells her: "Find the penknife . . . and plunge it / Into your false heart." The ballroom the lady has entered is "silent" and "empty," the mirror she looks into obscured by "cobwebs." She is in a state of despair brought on by internal desolation, and it is not unlikely that in depicting the lady's utter disenchantment, Auden has in mind the Kierkegaardian concept of dread. But it is clear that the lady in the poem has fooled herself in regard to her dual nature. The conflict between her ego and shadow, which she has discovered, has made her neurotic, her personality split (see Jung 1932, p. 341). An accommodation leading to love of her shadow side projected in the mirror could have avoided or healed the split. As the Jungian analyst Robert A. Johnson says, speaking in the context of romantic love, "We need to revere the unconscious parts of ourselves that we project. When we love our projections, when we honor our romantic ideals and fantasies, we affirm infinitely precious dimensions of our total selves" (1983, p. 194). The lady in the poem fails to do this.

While I doubt Auden intends to suggest suicide as a solution to the problem of neurosis, the suicide in the poem, given the fairy-tale setting, is an appropriate way for the lady with the "false heart" to die. Having failed to integrate the shadow into a viable relationship with her consciousness, the lady can hardly expect to find fulfillment in love, symbolized by the animus for a woman. On the fairy-tale level, her life ends in failure.

On a first reading, "Atlantis" seems a retelling of the traditional quest in a modern context. But, as Fuller points out, "the poem is addressed to a personal friend . . . and thus its admonitions acquire a certain concern, even a kind of charm" (1970, p. 180). Nevertheless, the retelling of the tale, as all retellings of the quest must be, is archetypal. Atlantis itself is an excellent symbol for the goal: a citadel of the Self. The mythical city stands for the uniting of the unconscious with the conscious, the excitement of questing for the unknown through our conscious knowledge of the traditional path.

Auden sets the informal tone and the modern context in the first stanza:

> Being set on the idea
>   Of getting to Atlantis,
> You have discovered of course
>   Only the Ship of Fools is
> Making the voyage this year,
>   As gales of abnormal force
>   Are predicted, and that you
>   Must therefore be ready to
> Behave absurdly enough
>   To pass for one of The Boys,
> At least appearing to love
>   Hard liquor, horseplay and noise.
>
>   (1979, p. 116)

The Ship of Fools is, of course, a microcosm, indicating that the journey is one everyman can make. And, although one may have "To pass for one of The Boys," one must ever be aware of the absurdity of denying one's true self for, as Auden's sonnet sequence, "The Quest," demonstrates, the goal is realization of the Self, that is, psychic wholeness.

There will be pessimists, "witty scholars, men / Who have proved there cannot be / Such a place as Atlantis" (ibid.). The quester is to take advantage of their knowledge, a knowledge based on the loss of a belief in the spiritual, in the power of myth and tradition. The poem's speaker notes that the "subtlety" of "their logic . . . betrays / Their enormous simple grief" (ibid., pp. 116–117), and I wonder if these lines refer indirectly to Auden's own loss and regaining of faith. Paradoxically, the quester learns from the pessimists "the ways / To doubt that you may believe" (ibid., p. 117). Here Jung's comment about doubt in his essay, "In Memory of Sigmund Freud," is apropos: "the nineteenth century has left us such a legacy of dubious propositions that doubt is not only possible but altogether justified, indeed meritorious. . . . Doubt alone is the mother of scientific truth" (1939, p. 47). One could say the same about the early twentieth century and conclude that doubt is also the mother of spiritual growth and belief.

In order that he may, again paradoxically, forget "completely /

About Atlantis," the quester is to "Strip off . . . [his] clothes and dance" (Auden 1979, p. 117) in a Dionysian frenzy in Thrace. Since the process of individuation is internal, clothes, symbol of one's persona, must be shed just as one's inhibitions must also be shed so that one may come in contact with the irrational, the unconscious shadow of this particular quester, to whom love of "Hard liquor, horseplay and noise" is alien.

After conscious contact with his shadow, the quester journeys to Carthage or Corinth (standing for hedonism according to Fuller (1970, p. 180)) where he encounters the archetypal temptress, a "tart" in "some bar" who offers him a "Counterfeit Atlantis," the recognition of which will enable him to know the real Atlantis when he sees it. In Jungian psychology, the temptress is the negative anima who would divert the man from his search for Selfhood.

Having successfully resisted the temptress, the questing hero is ready for a "terrible trek" through a wasteland of "squalid woods and frozen / Tundras where all are soon lost" (Auden 1979, p. 117). In this wasteland— like the descent into hell, a traditional symbol of the unconscious—the quester risks loss of consciousness. To save himself he is enjoined: "O remember the great dead / And honour the fate you are" (ibid., p. 118).[10] In other words, he must receive inspiration from and be guided by others who have completed the journey and by virtue of their success qualify as supraordinate personalities: symbols of the Selfhood the quester is seeking. Indeed, that Selfhood—the uniting of psychic opposites into a whole—is the "fate" he is.

Like the hero of "Atlantis," most of us never complete the individuation process. If, like Moses viewing the Promised Land from Pisgah, the quester is "allowed / Just to peep at Atlantis / In a poetic vision," he should "Give thanks and lie down in peace, / Having seen . . . [his] salvation (ibid.). He is very fortunate indeed to have achieved even a glimpse of Selfhood.

Auden ends the gentle satire of the poem with a note of encouragement: ". . . say / Good-bye now, and put to sea. / Farewell, my dear, farewell."[11] The speaker invokes the "Ancient of Days" to

Provide for all you must do
His invisible guidance,
Lifting up, dear, upon you
The light of His countenance.

(Ibid.)

Fittingly, Auden ends with an image of God, symbol of the wholeness and perfect unity of the Self.

Spender once wrote that Auden "consciously invents dreams and depicts actuality in the language of unconscious fantasies" (1953, p. 34). This, it seems to me, is what Auden has done in "Lady Weeping at the Crossroads" and "Atlantis." Drawing on fairy tales, myths, modern philosophy, and archetypal symbols, chief among them love, Auden offers in these and the other poems I have discussed, segments of the archetypal quest for individuation so necessary for psychic health in this Age of Anxiety.

Notes

1. Some of the other titles relevant to this study are: Freud, *Collected Works*; Blake, *Collected Works*; D. H. Lawrence, *Psycho-analysis and the Unconscious*, *Fantasia of the Unconscious*, and *Studies in Classical American Literature*; Homer Lane, *Talks to Parents and Teachers*; and Maud Bodkin, *Archetypal Patterns in Poetry*. The article, "Psychology and Art To-Day," was published in Geoffrey Grigson, ed., *The Arts To-Day* (London: John Lane The Bodley Head, 1935), pp. 1–21 (Callan 1983, pp. 269–270). In addition to this evidence, Auden's biographer, editor, and literary executor, Edward Mendelson, assures me that Auden was reading Jung extensively four years after this article was published (letter to the author, January 30, 1989).

2. See, for example, Callan (1965, 1977–1978, and 1983) and Charles Howard Long (1974). In "W. H. Auden's First Dramatization of Jung," Callan notes that Auden "found Freud's views on art and artistic creativity less convincing that Jung's accounts of the emergence of creature consciousness – the truly human quality – from the primal core of the libido" (1977–1978, p. 301).

3. Late in 1939 Auden wrote to a friend in England that America "has taught me the kind of writer I am, i.e. an introvert who can only develop by obeying his introversion" (1977, p. xx).

4. "A foolish consistency," said Emerson, "is the hobgoblin of little minds," and Auden, like most great writers, was certainly inconsistent. An example is the one letter I received from him (dated April 12, 1972, from 77 St. Mark's Place, New York City). As a young graduate student and aspiring poet at the University of New Mexico, I had sent him some of my poems and praised some of his which I'd read in the Modern Library edition, *Selected Poems*. Among the poems I praised were "The Unknown Citizen," "Lay your sleeping head, my love," and, I think, "*Musée des Beaux Arts*." I also praised "A Day for a Lay," an artful and amusing pornographic poem I'd read in *Avant Garde* (no doubt the publication of this poem was unauthorized; for a discussion of it, see Osborne 1979, pp. 283–284). Finally, I praised Auden's review of *The Letters of A. E. Housman*, which had appeared in *The New Yorker* (February 19, 1972) and which was later reprinted as "A Worcestershire Lad" in *Forewords and Afterwords* (1973, pp. 325–332). In the Housman review, Auden had referred to his fascination with Housman's "descriptions" of "the minor headaches which plague an author's life," such as "strangers" writing "who hardly ever enclose postage stamps" (Auden 1973, pp. 330–331). Since I'd written to Auden once before without receiving an answer, this time I enclosed a self-addressed, stamped envelope. That apparently, as they say, "did the trick." Here is the text of the letter I received:

> Dear Mr. Snider:
> Thank you for your letters. Glad you liked my Houseman [sic] piece.
> A word of advice: when singling out for praise a poem or two by another poet be careful not to choose one of his old war-horses to be

found in all anthologies. (Anthologists are incredibly lazy.) The poems may be good, but the author does not want to hear of them again.

I leave next Saturday for Austria where I have a summer home.
With best wishes
Yours sincerely
W. H. Auden
© 1989 The Estate of W. H. Auden

Naturally, I was thrilled to hear from the great man, whose work, I admit, I had not yet read widely and in depth. Today I understand why he would be offended by my praise of some of his early poems: most creative people are more excited about and prefer praise for their recent productions. Characteristically, his reply to me took the form of "laying down the law," to use Rowse's phrase (1987, p. 11). The joke is that he himself was an anthologist. Among the anthologies he edited are *The Poet's Tongue* (mentioned above) and *The Oxford Book of Light Verse* (1938). The obvious inconsistency is that one of the poems I had praised, "A Day for a Lay" (which Auden called "The Platonic Blow" (Osborne 1979, p. 283)), was and is not to be found in *any* anthology that I am aware of.

5. I have chosen to refer to the Vintage edition of Auden's *Selected Poems* because it is the most readily available and because it contains the early versions of the poems and some, such as "September 1, 1939," which Auden, unwisely I think, rejected from his canon.

6. For example, on June 28, 1935, not long before the Nazis enacted their anti-Jewish "Nuremberg" laws, "stringent new laws concerning homosexual conduct among men were promulgated" by the Nazis in Germany (Plant 1986, p. 69). These laws led to the deaths of tens of thousands of homosexuals in Nazi death camps (ibid., p. 149). Louis Crompton notes: "In England, arrests for homosexual offenses, which had averaged about 800 a year before World War II, rose to 3,000 in 1952" (1985, p. 376). Not until 1967, some six years before Auden's death, was homosexuality decriminalized in England (ibid., p. 377).

   Robert K. Martin writes: "That homosexuals can make their love poetry universal by concealing the beloved is a frequent supposition: it has been expressed as a desirable goal by Auden" (1979, p. 108).

7. Some Hindus apparently believe much the same. Auden's close friend and collaborator, Christopher Isherwood, describes how when he met the man who became his guru, Swami Prabhavananda, Isherwood wanted to know how he could lead a "spiritual life as long as . . . [he was] having a sexual relationship with a young man" (Isherwood 1980, p. 25). The Swami's answer was: "You must try to see him as the young Lord Krishna." The idea was that by seeing in the young man he loved the "young Lord Krishna," Isherwood would eventually see the spiritual beauty in Krishna and, if he were successful, Isherwood would "lose all desire for . . . [the young man's] body" (ibid.).

8. On a summer evening in June 1933, Auden seems to have had a mystical

"vision of Agape" himself. In "The Protestant Mystics," he quotes from "an unpublished account for the authenticity of which I can vouch." Mendelson believes the account relates Auden's own experience (Auden 1977, p. xvi). According to the account, Auden was sitting with "three colleagues, two women and one man . . . [who] were certainly not intimate friends, nor had any one of us a sexual interest in another." Then

> quite suddenly and unexpectedly, something happened. I felt myself invaded by a power which, though I consented to it, was irresistible and certainly not mine. For the first time in my life I knew exactly — because, thanks to the power, I was doing it — what it means to love one's neighbor as oneself. . . . My personal feelings towards them [his colleagues] were unchanged . . . but I felt their existence as themselves to be of infinite value and rejoiced in it. (Auden 1973, p. 69)

What Auden describes is the experience of becoming possessed, as it were, by an archetype, here the archetype of love in the form of Agape. This experience, or something very like it, must have suggested, consciously or unconsciously, the idea behind his famous line: "We must love one another or die." Auden may also have been thinking of Jung's comment in *Two Essays on Analytical Psychology*: "If men can be educated to see the shadow-side of their nature clearly, it may be hoped that they will also learn to understand and love their fellow men better" (1953, p. 36).

9. See Allen (1971, pp. 169–173 and 182–183). Allen includes "Lady Weeping at the Crossroads" in his section titled "The Double," thereby implying the poem treats accommodation with the shadow.

10. Auden subsequently revised the first of these two lines to read: "Remember the noble dead" (1966, p. 203). The newer line has a smoother, more pleasing, rhythm and drops the rather quaint sounding "O."

11. Auden later changed "my dear" to "dear friend." He also changed "dear" in the penultimate line to "friend" (1966, p. 204). The changes, I think, make the tone ever so slightly more personal and less satirical.

Works Cited

Allen, John Alexander, ed. 1971. *Hero's Way: Contemporary Poems in the Mythic Tradition*. Englewood Cliffs, N.J.: Prentice.

Auden, W. H. 1966. *Collected Shorter Poems: 1927–1957*. New York: Vintage.

———. 1961. The Quest Hero. *The Texas Quarterly* 4:81–93.

———. 1970. "A Day for a Lay." *Avant Garde* (March):46–47.

———. 1973. *Forewords and Afterwords*. New York: Vintage.

———. 1977. *The English Auden: Poems, Essays, and Dramatic Writings, 1927–1939*. Edward Mendelson, ed. New York: Random.

———. 1979. *Selected Poems*. New edition. Edward Mendelson, ed. New York: Vintage.

Callan, Edward. 1965. Allegory in Auden's *The Age of Anxiety*. *Twentieth Century Literature* 10:155–165.

———. 1977–1978. W. H. Auden's first dramatization of Jung: the charade of the loving and terrible mothers. *Comparative Drama* 11:287–302.

———. 1983. *Auden: A Carnival of Intellect*. New York: Oxford University Press.

Carpenter, Humphrey. 1981. *W. H. Auden: A Biography*. Boston: Houghton.

Crompton, Louis. 1985. *Byron and Greek Love: Homophobia in 19th-Century England*. Berkeley, Calif.: University of California Press.

Foote, Timothy. 1973. Auden: the sage of anxiety. *Time*, October 8, 1973, pp. 113–114.

Fuller, John. 1970. *A Reader's Guide to W. H. Auden*. New York: Farrar.

Isherwood, Christopher. 1937. Some notes on Auden's early poetry. *New Verse* (November 1937):4–9. Reprinted in *Auden: A Collection of Critical Essays*, Monroe K. Spears, ed. (Englewood Cliffs, N.J.: Prentice, 1964), pp. 10–14.

———. 1980. *My Guru and His Disciple*. New York: Farrar.

Johnson, Robert A. 1983. *WE: Understanding the Psychology of Romantic Love*. San Francisco: Harper.

Jung, C. G. 1931. On the relation of analytical psychology to poetry. *CW* 15:65–83. Princeton, N.J.: Princeton University Press, 1966.

———. 1932. Psychotherapists or the clergy. *CW* 11:327–347. Princeton, N.J.: Princeton University Press, 1958.

———. 1939. In memory of Sigmund Freud. *CW* 15:41–51. Princeton, N.J.: Princeton University Press, 1966.

———. 1946. The fight with the shadow. *CW* 10:218–226. Princeton, N.J.: Princeton University Press, 1964.

———. 1950. Psychology and literature. *CW* 15:84–107. Princeton, N.J.: Princeton University Press, 1966.

_____. 1953. *Two Essays on Analytical Psychology*. R. F. C. Hull, trans. New York: World.

Kroll, Jack. 1973. W. H. Auden: mapping the twentieth century. *Newsweek*, October 8, 1973, p. 117.

Long, Charles Howard. 1974. The quest dialectic: the Jungian and Kierkegaardian quest for unity in W. H. Auden's "The Quest," *New Year Letter*, and *For the Time Being*. DAI 34: 5187A.

Martin, Robert K. 1979. *The Homosexual Tradition in American Poetry*. Austin: University of Texas Press.

Mendelson, Edward. 1981. *Early Auden*. New York: Viking.

Osborne, Charles. 1979. *W. H. Auden: The Life of a Poet*. New York: Harcourt.

Plant, Richard. 1986. *The Pink Triangle: The Nazi War Against Homosexuals*. New York: Henry Holt.

Rowse, A. L. 1987. *The Poet Auden: A Personal Memoir*. New York: Weidenfeld and Nicolson.

Spender, Stephen. 1953. W. H. Auden and his poetry. *The Atlantic Monthly* 192:74–79. Reprinted in *Auden: A Collection of Critical Essays*, Monroe K. Spears, ed. (Englewood Cliffs, N.J.: Prentice, 1964), pp. 26–38.

Index

"A Dialogue Between the Soul and the Body" (Marvel), 25 n.8
Adler, Alfred, 2
Agape, 133–141 *passim*
  in Auden's experience, 147–148 n.8
AIDS, 119, 122–123
Aiken, Conrad, 87
  review of *Orlando*, 87
Androgyny
  in Carson McCullers, *The Member of the Wedding*, 109
  in Virginia Woolf, 87–104 *passim*
Anima, the, 5, 14, 15ff, 33
  in Auden, 141
  in *Orlando* and *The Waves*, 87–104 *passim*
  in *The Picture of Dorian Gray*, 78–79
  in *Tristram of Lyonesse*, 45–69 *passim*
Animus, the, 5, 14, 15ff
  in Auden, 141, 144
  in *Orlando* and *The Waves*, 87–104 *passim*
  in *Tristram of Lyonesse*, 45–69 *passim*
Antihero
  Frankie Adams as, 111, 113
  Holden Caulfield as, 111
Anti-Semitism (Nazi laws against Jews), 147 n.6
Aphrodite, 133
Archetypal criticism, 1, 4–7
  partial bibliography of, xi
Archetypes
  compensatory nature of, xi–xii, 6, 132, 133, 139–140
  defined, 2–3, 4–5
  dual nature of, 3
    in *Dorian Gray*, 81, 82–83
  literary critics moved by, 7
Arnold, Matthew, 7, 32–33

Merlin in, 32–33
Tristram and Iseult, 32–33, 62
Arthur, King, 20, 30
  in Tennyson, 34–35
Atlantis, as symbol for the Self, 142–143
Attitude types. *See* Psychological types
Auden, W. H., xii, 11
  "A Day for a Lay" ("The Platonic Blow"), 146 n.4
  "Archaelogy," 140–141
    shadow and history in, 140
  archetype of love in, 133–145 *passim*
  "Atlantis," 11, 141, 142–145
    as symbol for the Self, 140
    negative anima in, 144
    revisions of, 148 n.10 and n.11
  "August 1968," 140
    collective shadow in, 140
  awareness of Jung, 129ff
  describes himself as
    an introvert, 146, n.3
    thinking-intuitive type, 129
  experience of Agape, 147–148 n.8
  heterosexuality and, 135–136
  homosexuality and, 134, 135–137, 147 n.7
  ideas about creativity vs. Jung, 130ff, 146–147 n.4
  influence of myth on, 130
  "In Memory of Sigmund Freud" (contrasted with Jung), 131–133
  "In Memory of W. B. Yeats," 132, 133
  "Lady Weeping at the Crossroads," 141–142, 145
    accommodating the shadow in, 141–142